Escape From Debtors Prison

Got MONEY?

1st of the Series

Rachelle & Tyrone Potts, C.P.A.

All paraphrased quotations are the authors' added emphasis.

Escape From Debtors Prison: Got MONEY?

For information regarding presentations or products, call or write:
Prosperity Outpouring To The Saints, International (POTTS, Intl.)
Tyrone and Rachelle Potts
(310) 542-5001
e-mail: hisfavor@aol.com
www.prosperityoutpouring.qpg.com

ISBN: 0-9701780-0-X
Printed in the United States of America

El Shaddai Publishing
Post Office Box 13921
Torrance, CA 90503

Cover design by Carl Moore, visionarygraphix@mediaone.net

Contents

Dedication

This book is dedicated to the memory of my grandfather, Austin "Boo" Joseph, Sr. As the patriarchal provider of my family, he personified faithfulness, unconditional love and generosity. I am eternally grateful to God for allowing him to pivotally influence my upbringing. He instilled in me core values and the belief that there is nothing I cannot do, for this he was, is, and will forever be my beloved "Dadda."

Rachelle Potts

This book is also dedicated to the thousands of people who are sick and tired of being sick and tired, those who are ready to do whatever it takes to obtain permanent, financial independence.

Tyrone Potts

Acknowledgments

We would like to extend our gratitude to the following people for their wisdom, guidance, love and continued support of us completing this labor of love. Your help is much appreciated and your kindness will never be forgotten.

Bishop Charles E. Blake's teaching has shaped and transformed our lives tremendously. Despite the demands of his hectic schedule he made time to write a poignant foreword to our book.

Darnell and Deborah Pegues, our mentors, have given us practical advice, constructive criticism and spiritual motivation. They've extended opportunities that may not have otherwise been afforded us.

Elder Hammonds has been our teacher, role model, friend and spiritual father. He laid the scriptural foundation for the successful, abundant life we base our ministry upon.

Dr. Paredes' dedication to minister healing to the wounded in the Body of Christ has inspired us to do the same. It is a privilege to be trained by one of God's finest.

Kecia Ephriam set aside many hours of her life to prayerfully join her faith with ours. She blessed us immensely.

Carl and Edmarine Moore went far beyond the call of duty. They unselfishly opened their home and their hearts to us.

Our family and friends understood our need to be in seclusion for three months without complaining (much). We love you.

Foreword By Bishop Charles E. Blake

Spiritual health and prosperity is my prayer for all Christians. When the spirit of a person is whole, the other aspects of life can be managed more effectively. God's Word relays concern for every spiritual, natural and physical area in the human experience.

The Potts have written a book that addresses one of the most important areas that all people must deal with everyday: management of financial resources. They offer practical information to be utilized by Christians who desire to improve their quality of life, and become better stewards of the resources that God provides.

Freedom from financial bondage requires access to accurate information and a personal commitment to discontinue destructive behaviors. *Got MONEY?* gives instruction, insight, and a wealth of immediately useful "tools" that can help develop discipline for a new start toward prosperity.

Bishop Charles E. Blake, Pastor
West Angeles Church of God In Christ, Los Angeles
Southern California First Jurisdictional Prelate
1st Assistant to the Presiding Bishop of the C.O. G. I. C.
Author of *Free to Dream!*

Preface By Dr. Mardra J. Paredes

Financial struggles are noted among couples as one of the top three sources of marital discord. Financial distress is a leading cause of depression among economically impoverished individuals. Inadequate finances have been used by a number of criminals as an excuse to rob and steal. We could surmise that financial difficulties have a direct correlation to a variety of intrapersonal and interpersonal conflicts.

Minister Tyrone Potts and his lovely wife, Evangelist Rachelle Potts of Prosperity Outpouring To The Saints International teach us how to accelerate our way out of debt, plan our future, make our money work for us, work smarter not harder and so much more.

As a psychotherapist and director of a Counseling Center, I highly recommend this wonderful book as a book of knowledge. Ecclesiastes 7:12 reads, "For wisdom is a defense, and money is a defense; but the excellency of knowledge is that wisdom giveth life to them that have it." Got MONEY? provides knowledge to create and preserve prosperity. Buy it, read it, apply the principles and you will be blessed.

Mardra J. Paredes, Ph.D.
Director of Counseling Services
West Angeles Church of God in Christ
Founder of MP Counseling, Los Angeles

Preface by Elder Kenneth Hammonds

I was thrilled to be among the first to review what I knew would be exciting literature. Well, I was not disappointed. This is a fine work, but not for the financially timid or tenderhearted. *Got MONEY?* moves you beyond Total Indulgence and Debtors Prison to financial freedom.

I've known this young spiritual couple for a number of years. I watched Tyrone grow and participated in some of his lively discussions, like God does not want Christians to have ANY debt. To some these discussions seemed impossible and certainly not what the "average Joe" could or even should do in debt-ridden America. But when Tyrone began to share how he applied God's Word to eliminate $100,000 of debt in three years on one income, suddenly everyone was listening. *Got MONEY?* will get your attention.

I met Rachelle when she attended the School of Success (SOS) at West Angeles Church of God in Christ in Los Angeles. Wow, what a determined and insightful woman of God. Now the two are married and presenting a powerful ministry of financial freedom for the Body of Christ. The principles of P.O.T.T.S., Intl. are profound and biblical. The Potts present a powerful dynamic duo of insight and practical hints for living a purposeful Christian life.

Got MONEY? is the first book of the "Escape From Debtors Prison" series. It gives great insight into money and successful living. Full of information and documentation, the Potts charge the Body of Christ to become the people God called them to be. The stories and illustrations are truly inspiring. You'll be challenged to seek God to understand the proper place of money in your life.

Dr. Kenneth Hammonds, M.Div., Ed D.
Personal Success & Leadership Coach
Author of *God Wants You To Be Wealthy*

Introduction

Beloved, I pray that you may prosper in all things and be in health, just as your soul prospers. 3 John 2

Approximately 10:40 A.M. she awakened at the sound of blue birds singing outside her window. She sat up in her stadium sized bed, took off her satin eye mask and casually reached over with her right hand and picked up a tiny crystal bell which rang gingerly at the touch of her finger tips. The French double doors burst opened and her servants poured into her boudoir before she could sit the bell back down on the bed stand. One servant went straight over to the bed and placed her slippers on her feet before they touched the floor. Another servant went into her private salon and began drawing her a warm bath seasoned with natural salts and herbs, topped with fresh rose petals. One servant opened the drapes on the east wing to let in some sunlight, while another stood next to the bed helping her put on her bath robe. Two more servants started dusting and replacing her one-night-old bedding with new silk linens. She was presented with both fresh flowers and warm towels before her eyes fully opened. But to her, this day was just another Tuesday.

I imagine this to be a typical morning for Elizabeth, Queen of England, at the renown Buckingham Palace. But, how many of us ever fathom living such a lavish, regal lifestyle. Most see this as unrealistic as the fairy tales we read when we were children. For years we played games in which our roles were king and queen or prince and princess. When we matured the world informed us that no "average Joe" could possibly live this way. Only the rich and famous experienced this level of abundance. As spectators we rush to witness the media's remote coverage of a royal wedding or an inaugural ball. We fantasize about positions of great power and prominence, wondering what it feels like to be sovereign. Yet deep down we are resolved with the fact that this is how the other half, the better half lives.

Instead we drudgingly arise early in the morning, drag ourselves to jobs we hate, spending 8 or 9 plus hours earning less money than we deserve only to return home exhausted and afraid to answer our own telephone for fear that another creditor is calling to collect on a past due bill. Day after day, week after week, month after month and year after year we repeat this most dishonoring cycle of despair, sometimes never realizing that we are living far beneath the privilege that God has provided for us. We are locked up; incarcerated in a minimum security prison for life. Everyday we go out on our work release programs. But, we are unable to enjoy the fruits of our labor. In short, debtors' prison follows the familiar tune, 'Hi Hoe' from the popular tale, *Snow White and the Seven Dwarfs*.

I owe I owe So off to work I go

Wish I could drop But, I can't stop

Cause I owe I owe I owe I owe

This book is written out of a righteous indignation against the way Christians live in today's society. We are God's people. We are royalty. So, why do we live like peasants? Some do not know where their next meal is coming from. Others live from paycheck to paycheck. God forbid they find themselves jobless without a moments notice. In many cases they are just one paycheck away from homelessness. It has become increasingly difficult to distinguish a Christian from someone who does not know Christ. This should not be.

At the dawning of the 21st century, a new millennium, we believe that anyone can accomplish whatever he or she works toward. We are not trapped in a socialist or communist society where our potential is limited by national controls. Capitalism encourages us to strive for the American dream: "life, liberty and the pursuit of happiness." For many that American dream has become a recurring nightmare with the bars and chains of bondage characterized by debt. Many feel like they are drowning, unable to keep their heads above water. They do not hear God speaking to them, because their bills are crying louder and demanding their attention. Have Americans become so preoccupied with comfort and convenience that they've made themselves miserable?

"More than ever before, pastors and evangelists are teaching the biblical principles of prosperity which include the tithe, offering, seed time and harvest time. Click on any popular television ministry and you're likely to hear the gospel of abundance and testimonies of those who have been set free from money worries," says Veronica Mackey, staff writer for the Los Angeles Wave newspaper in October 1999 article entitled, "Prosperity Is Not A Concept For Christians To Shun." Jesus Christ clearly expounds that He came to earth so that Christians would live prosperous lives. "*The thief does not come except to steal, and to kill and to destroy. I have come that they may have life, and that they may have it more abundantly" (John 10:10).*

Although prosperity teaching is essential, there appears to be a lack of instruction in the area of stewardship, application and empowerment with regard to finances. God does work miracles in the financial realm. There is no question of God's ability to prosper his people. Deuteronomy 8:18 says, *"And you shall remember the Lord your God, for it is He who gives you power to get wealth, that He may establish His covenant which He swore to your fathers, as it is this day."* What are we doing to show God that he can trust us with wealth? Matthew 25:14-30 accounts the Parable of the Talents, "*You were faithful over few things, I will make you ruler over many things"(Matthew 25:21).*

We sit in the plush pews of our beautiful sanctuaries. Our excitement soars when the prosperity preacher comes to town. The message is usually; 'Name it, Claim it, Blab it and Grab it!' The preacher proclaims, 'Riches are ours!' We get so entranced and swept up in a world-wind of hope, we seldom realize that we have returned to our homes without the practical tools we need to make that transfer of wealth happen. We are missing the most significant part of the process. "*Thus also faith by itself, if it does not have works, is dead" (James 2:17).* The Southern California Christian Times, Orange and Los

Angeles County Edition posted this announcement in November 1999:

> HARTFORD, Conn. (EP) - When Norman and Melissa Cameron stopped making payments on their Hartford, Connecticut house, the Federal National Mortgage Association (FNMA) began foreclosure proceedings. The Camerons contacted FNMA officials to explain why they had stopped making payments on their $54,000 mortgage: God told them they could. "It was our desire to be free from this mortgage debt," the Camerons told the court overseeing the foreclosure. "Therefore we asked God our Heavenly Father in the name of Jesus Christ. He heard us and He freed us from this mortgage bondage." FNMA officials will continue with foreclosure proceedings until they, too, are contacted by God.

Obviously, something is missing. "*But do you want to know, O foolish man, that faith without works is dead? You see then that a man is justified by works, and not by faith only" (James 2:20,24).* Diligence is required.

This book will give you every tool you need to build and maintain wealth. We help you to develop the right attitude toward money by teaching you the true value and purpose of money as an instrument that should work for you. Reading will help you identify how you fell into debt and clear up common misconceptions many form about money. We uncover the hidden pitfalls to every method of obtaining money. Anyone can acquire the dollars and sense necessary to reach his or her full financial potential. *Got Money?* will empower you to produce wealth and to refrain from the gross consumption of income. We parallel our daily lives with the struggles of the Israelites, God's chosen people. These pages reveal the secrets to building your personal empire and establishing a dynasty of economic abundance. It is time Christians stop following the world and lead a financial revolution. Let us step into our royal roles. After all, we are children of the King, heirs of the kingdom. You have in your hands the wisdom and authority to overturn your life sentence to Debtors Prison and to pave your way to glorious financial freedom.

While the content of this book is ours together, areas that contain statistical data, financial calculations and analyses are written by Tyrone Potts, otherwise the voice is Rachelle Potts'.

Chapter 1

Money: A Means To An End

...But money answers everything. Ecclesiasties 10:19

My nephew, Marcus, became the best trader on the New Hampshire lunch exchange. At 12:00 noon the lunch bell rang at New Hampshire elementary school. Jesse rushed into the cafeteria. He was especially excited because it was Thursday, which meant the main course was pizza. After Jesse obtained his tray of goodies he looked around the room until he spotted Marcus, his best friend, seated at a table near the window. Jesse then proceeded to the table and sat facing Marcus. Marcus etched out a smile, but Jesse noticed that something seemed to be bothering Marcus.

"What's wrong?" Jesse asked his homeroom buddy.

Marcus opened his lunch box packed by his mom from home. Inside was a peanut butter and jelly sandwich, cookies, a bag of potato chips and a granny green apple. Jesse immediately knew what was bugging Marcus.

Jesse said, "She gave you peanut butter and jelly again! Haven't you told her that you're tired of having that for lunch? Why don't you make her give you something else."

Marcus gave Jesse the most sarcastic look he could muster and replied, "Make her! Have you met my mom?"

Jesse responded apologetically, "Oh, sorry. I won't give up my pizza for your sandwich. However, I am interested in those cookies and that bag of potato chips," Jesse continued.

A mysterious smile crept across Marcus' face and he answered in his best Godfather impersonation, "Make me an offer I can't refuse."

Jesse giggled at Marcus' comedic gesture and replied, "Okay, I'll give you my french fries, they're not as crispy as I like them anyway." Marcus in turn agreed to trade Jesse his potato chips for the fries.

While the two ate and began to make plans for the weekend, another classmate named Sally approached the table and sat next to Marcus. Sally was extremely health conscious for a third grader. She stared across the table at Jesse and began to make weird facial expressions as she watched him gobble bite after bite of his pizza. Jesse noticed Sally's distracting gaze and reluctantly asked her why she wasn't eating. Sally responded with her oral dissertation on how fat, grease and cholesterol clog your arteries and kill you. Jesse bluntly interrupted her.

"Sally, you are eight years old, for goodness sake. You don't have to worry about stuff like that until you're at least forty. Then you're about to die anyway so it really doesn't matter." Jesse continued, "If you don't want to eat your lunch, I'll gladly take it off your hands." Jesse reached across the table to grab Sally's plate, but she guarded it with her arms.

"Not so fast," she said, "I'll give you my pizza for your garden salad. I have to eat something you know."

Jesse squealed, "Here, by all means take the salad. I don't know why they bother putting it on my plate anyway. Yuck!"

Sally turned to Marcus, who was still eating Jesse's french fries, and smiled. "I see that you like fries so I saved mine for you." Marcus took Sally's fries, murmured a thanks and continued eating. Marcus was careful not to give Sally much attention because the entire class knew she had a crush on him.

Moments before the bell sounded, which ended lunch and prompted the kids back to class, Sidney entered. The lunch line had already closed. Sidney arrived too late to be served. He rushed over to Marcus, who always had a peanut butter and jelly sandwich to spare.

"Please give me your sandwich?" Sidney begged.

"No way!" Marcus responded.

Jesse and Sally watched in amazement, because they both knew that Marcus had no intention of eating that sandwich. Marcus and Sidney argued back and forth for at least three minutes until Sidney desperately pulled out a crisp \$5 bill. "Here Marcus," he said, "I missed breakfast and now I'm too late for lunch. I had planned to buy myself some snacks after school, but I am starving now."

Marcus complied without hesitation. He placed the \$5 bill in his pocket while he and Jesse walked out of the cafeteria. As the two strolled down the corridor, Marcus opened and finally began to eat his package of cookies. Jesse went to the rest room and Marcus called home from the pay telephone in the hallway. He left his mother the message, "Thanks for the peanut butter and jelly sandwich. Don't forget to make me another one tomorrow." When Marcus entered his classroom he presented his teacher with a granny green apple. She was delighted and hoped that the rest of the class would learn to be as considerate and as generous as her model student, Marcus.

...And a little child shall lead them. Isaiah 11:6

Origins of the Monetary System

Before 700 B.C. there was no known existence of money in the form of currency.[1] Bartering was man's only means of obtaining property and other possessions since the

---

[1] Tenney, Merrill C.

1963 *The Zondervan Pictorial Bible Dictionary*: Michigan: Zondervan Publishing House: page 551.

beginning of civilization. People simply traded one thing for another without the exchange of money. The barter system became extremely inefficient because it required that one locate a person who wanted what he provided, and coincidentally happened to have available for exchange a product he wanted. In a rapidly growing population, one would have to execute an extensive search in order to locate such a person.[2] Society was forced to find a more efficient means of obtaining both the necessities and the desires of life. Hence, the barter-method was followed by the weight system, later by minted coins, paper money, until today we have the credit system by which one may live, buy, and sell without the use of money at all.[3]

History of Currency

In 1792 the American government adopted the U.S. dollar.[4] Although getting Americans accustomed to this new monetary system was no easy task, it was an essential one. Money is one of the most important inventions of humankind. Without it a complex, modern economy based on the division of labor, and the consequent widespread exchange of goods and services, would be impossible.[5]

Today's society would be completely lost without this thing we call money. Originally money was guaranteed by the value of a commodity such as gold or silver. In the late 19th

---

[2] Mayer, Thomas
1993 Money: Grolier Electronic Publishing, Inc: page 1.
[3] Tenney, Merrill C.
1963 *The Zondervan Pictorial Bible Dictionary*: Michigan: Zondervan Publishing House: page 551.
[4] Aubrey, Henry G.
1993 Dollar: Grolier Electronic Publishing, Inc: page 1.
[5] Mayer, Thomas
1993 Money: Grolier Electronic Publishing, Inc: page 1.

and early 20th centuries, most western countries based their currencies on gold. This was called the gold standard.[6] Now all U.S. money is credit money, or flat money; the guarantee no longer exists.

One might well ask why people are willing to exchange valuable goods and services for pieces of paper called $10 bills. The answer is that these pieces of paper are valuable because we know that other people are willing to take them in exchange for goods. The same is ultimately true of gold. It is considered valuable because we know that other people treat it as valuable. Hence, many of those who advocate a return to the gold standard do so primarily because this would limit the government's ability to create money rather than because of any inherent value attached to gold.[7] Contrary to popular belief, it does matter what other people think.

Functions of Money

Money has only three functions. It acts as a medium of exchange, a standard of value and a store of wealth. Unfortunately, we have placed more value on money than was ever intended.

A medium of exchange is simply an item used to make it easy to exchange things. In a very primitive economy, as we said, people directly bartered goods and services. The use of money as a medium of exchange allows us to split this barter process into two parts. All we have to do is locate a person who wants our product, receive money in exchange for it, and then locate another person who has available the product we want and who is willing to take money in payment for it.[8]

---

[6] Mayer, Thomas
1993 Money: Grolier Electronic Publishing, Inc: page 2.
[7] Ibid. page 3.
[8] Mayer, Thomas

Another function of money is to serve as a standard of value or unit of account so that economic values in terms of money can be measured; in this respect, money serves as an abstract unit.[9] This standard of value function is overwhelmingly important because a modern economy requires numerous comparisons of values. This function of money helps to ensure that individuals receive fair market value in exchange for goods and services.

The third function of money is to serve as a store of wealth. This is not a distinctive function of money, but money has certain peculiarities as a store of wealth. Unlike other forms of wealth, it has no transactions costs. Someone who decides to hold wealth in corporate stock, for example, has to undergo a certain amount of trouble and cost, first to buy stock and then to sell it again in order to buy another item. All of these costs and inconveniences can be avoided by holding one's wealth in the form of money. Economists term this ease of using money, as opposed to other forms of wealth, as liquidity.[10]

Cash should always be held in a secure location to insure its benefit. Stuffing considerable amounts of money in a cookie jar or stashing large chunks of money in a mattress is unsafe. The threat of someone burglarizing your home to steal hidden money is small compared to what you lose by just having it sit.

Money held outside an investment vehicle is stolen by time. This process is called the decline or loss of purchase power. *Webster's* defines *inflation* as a substantial and continuing rise in the general price level. According to a study performed by Ibbotson Associates in 1999, the rate of inflation

---

1993 Money: Grolier Electronic Publishing, Inc: page 1.

[9] Ibid. page 2.

[10] Mayer, Thomas

1993 Money: Grolier Electronic Piblishing, Inc: page 1.

averaged roughly 3% over the last seventy-four years. Consequently, Margaret Moody,* a retired nurse, was astonished to find that the sure-footed thief, time had stolen half of her money.

In January 1980 she placed $5,000 of her savings in a strong box and buried it in her own back yard. Ms. Moody retrieved it in December 1999, to find that it is was worth roughly half its original value. She did not understand why an untouched, twenty-year-old dollar was now worth approximately fifty cents. How did this happen? The answer is inflation. In the United States, a capitalistic society, the profit motive tends to drive the prices for goods and services higher with the passage of time. This also makes the value of money decrease. A wise sage once expressed, "Time waits for no one." Ms. Moody learned this lesson the hard way. We race against time because as time lapses the market forces generally lead to inflation. If someone stands still in a race, he or she is automatically left behind.

We casually watch movies such as 'Back to the Future' and 'Blast from the Past,' in their portrayal of characters who find themselves in disarray when lost in an unfamiliar time. Similarly, our out-dated money is lost to a foreign future. We cannot resurrect money like a memento from a past decade and expect it to function up to par.

Had Margaret Moody intended to use her savings to help pay for her granddaughter's college education, the outcome would have been more devastating. Buying groceries at her neighborhood super market could become a trying experience as well. Both groceries and education cost are increasing faster than the rate of inflation. Not long ago $50 of groceries filled my basket and fed me for weeks. Now I spend three times that amount for less food, a perfect example of lost purchase power.

---

* Pseudonym

Bank of America, a conventional bank, offered a savings account that yielded a 1.01% return on the investment dollar as of April 30, 2000 (less after taxes). Because the rate of inflation has been approximately 3%, money is worth less and less. If we do not do something to outpace inflation, we are fighting a losing battle.

Table 1: Shows value of a 1926 dollar in future years*

Year	Value
1950	.50
1974	.25
1998	.13

* Assumes average inflation rate per year of 3.08%.

Chapter 2

Feast or Famine: Money Misconceptions

There is one who makes himself rich, yet has nothing,
And one who makes himself poor, yet has great riches.
Proverbs 8:18

Now that we have explained the origin, history and functions of money, it is time to take an honest look at the perceptions that have been formed concerning money. Two extremes exist: a feast mentality and a famine mentality. Both mentalities are frequently found in upper, middle and lower class America and both are detrimental.

Have you ever attended a feast? A feast is usually an elaborate banquet. The host or hostess serves many enticing delicacies and guests are entertained throughout the entire event. Feasts are primarily planned to celebrate the accomplishments of individuals, to mark holidays or to observe special occasions. Ordinarily guests attend by invitation only, because much time and preparation is vested in presenting a feast. Consequently, feasts do not happen everyday.

Total Indulgence Zero Guilt

A popular weight loss center once advertised its line of desserts with the slogan: 'Total indulgence zero guilt.' The center claimed, 'you could have your cake and eat it too.' Every time I saw their television commercial, which displayed tantalizing desserts from A to Z, a banana split began to call my name. It said to me, 'Come on, you know you want me. You only live once. Enjoy yourself, you deserve it! Eventually, I gave in.

The total indulgence theme rings true for feast mentality individuals. These people feast on a daily basis, not just special occasions. They live each day as if it were their last. Roland Dorsey* was one of these people. "Tomorrow is promised to no one," he always said, "so I might as well enjoy myself today." Why save for tomorrow, when I can have what I want right now? This single, thirty-seven-year-old salesman from New Jersey truly believed that *more is always better*. He chose to live an undisciplined lifestyle which indulged his every whim.

Roland never married. Although he dated spectacular women, Roland decided that he would not tie himself down to just one, because of course, *more is always better.*

Roland made a very good living. He was an extremely talented salesman. Annually, Roland earned six figures in commissions alone, not counting his base salary. God blessed Roland with the ability to sell sand in the desert at a premium.

To many Roland had more money than he knew what to do with. Often his money was already spent long before his paycheck arrived. Roland drove the best car. He wore the best suits. Once Roland spent over a thousand dollars on one pair of shoes. He spared no expense. Roland only ate at five star restaurants and he always ordered the most expensive item on the menu, whether he liked it or not.

Roland's home depicted his excessive lifestyle even further. Although he spent very little time at home, Roland chose to live in the most exclusive residential area he could find. He purchased top of the line furniture, appliances and every electronic device on the market. Roland accepted nothing but the best because, he truly believed that *more is always better.*

A feast mentality dictates living in excess. John 10:10b says, *"I have come that they may have life, and that they may*

---

* Pseudonym

have it more abundantly." There is a distinct difference between living in abundance and living in excess. God wants us to live in abundance, not excess.

Psalms 23:1 reads, "*The Lord is my shepherd, I shall not want.*" Abundant living is not wanting. A beautiful paradox is explained once you realize that delighting yourself in the Lord will result in His giving you the desires of your heart[1] (Psalm 37:4). Similarly, Psalm 84:11 assures, "*The Lord will give grace and glory; No good thing will He withhold from those who walk uprightly.*"

First Timothy 6:17 states, "*Command those who are rich in this present age not to be haughty, nor to trust in uncertain riches but in the living God, who gives us richly all things to enjoy.*" Riches are a responsibility. This verse clears up much misunderstanding about the acquisition or possession of material goods. Apostle Paul tells us not to trust in uncertain riches. Here, the word "trust" (Greek: *Elpizo*) means to expect them to bring us security or deliverance. Wise trusting lies in putting our hope in God alone. Further, we must never let the presence of wealth make us think that we are better than others or that we can be irresponsible or indulgent. It is a responsibility, a great responsibility, to have great wealth; and we must always remember "*To whom much is given, from him much will be required; and to whom much has been committed, of him they will ask the more*" (*Luke 12:48*).[2]

Jesus Christ himself presents us with the question, "*For what will it profit a man if he gains the whole world, and loses*

---

[1] Paraphrased Psalm 37:4 *Delight yourself also in the Lord,*
And He shall give you the desires of your heart.

[2] Price, Dr. Frederick K.C. 1992 Spirit Filled Life Study Bible: Kingdom Dynamics: Thomas Nelson Publishers: Nashville, TN: page 1848

his own soul?" (Mark 8:36). Clearly it is God's will that we possess our desires. It is not His will, however, that our desires possess us. Money is indeed a desired and needed possession. *Webster's Seventh New Collegiate Dictionary* defines *possession* as the act of having or taking into control. Feast mentality individuals must decide to take money (and other possessions) under their control as opposed to allowing it to control them. When one accomplishes this feat, he is well on his way to understanding abundant living.

Queen Marie Antoinette of France is a good representative of excessive, feast mentality living. She is noted for her pronouncement, "Let them eat cake." Living in excess is a wasteful, reckless and irresponsible use of the resources that God has entrusted to your care.

Moreover, excessive living is covetous conduct. *Webster's* defines *covetous* as marked by inordinate desire for wealth and possessions. Hebrews 13:5 says "*Let your conduct be without covetousness, be content with such things as you have.*" In other words, more is NOT always better.

Covetousness is driven by a spirit of lust. Unfortunately, lust is a thirst which can never be quenched; a desire that can never be fulfilled. Eventually lust can destroy its prey. "*There is a way that seems right to a man, but its end is the way of death" (Proverbs 14:12).*

Such was the case with Roland Dorsey. He died at age 37. Roland's heart collapsed because he would not alter his diet of rich, decadent foods. Although he saw the warning signs of his failing health, Roland refused to deprive himself of what he thought was the best. "*He who loves pleasure will be a poor man; He who loves wine and oil will not be rich" (Proverbs 21:17).*

Roland should have been a multi-millionaire, leaving a wealthy inheritance to his family. Instead he died alone and penniless. Roland was so deep in debt that all of his material possessions amounted to less than the obligations he had incurred with his creditors. *"He who trusts in his riches will fall, but the righteous will flourish like foliage" (Proverbs 11:28).*

Roland Dorsey's sixty-five-year-old, widowed mother was left with a hefty bill to settle Roland's estate. After spending all of her savings, she was forced to borrow money to bury her only son. Roland's mother decided to postpone her retirement so that she could pay back the loan and reestablish a savings.

If you have experienced any of the aforementioned feast mentality, excessive living symptoms, I have wonderful news. Approximately 931 B.C. the Great Physician wrote a prescription for your condition. Vaccinate yourself with the biblical book, Ecclesiastes and you will be cured. Until you experience permanent relief, continue to take these verses:

"I made my works great, I built myself houses, and planted myself vineyards. I made myself gardens and orchards, and I planted all kinds of fruit trees in them. I made myself water pools from which to water the growing trees of the grove. I acquired male and female servants, and had servants born in my house...I also gathered for myself silver and gold and the special treasures of kings and of provinces. I acquired male and female singers, the delights of the sons of men, and musical instruments of all kinds. So I became great and excelled more than all who were before me...Whatever my eyes desired I did not keep from them. I did not withhold my heart from any pleasure, for my heart rejoiced in all my labor; and this was my reward from all my labor. Then I looked on all the works that my hands had done And the labor in which I had toiled; And indeed all was vanity and grasping for the wind. There was no profit under the sun" (Ecclesiasties 2:4-11). "He who loves silver will not be satisfied with silver" (Ecclesiasties 5:10a).

Rolands are a dime a dozen. Many unemployed individuals and welfare recipients share his feast mentality. They make comments like, "If I were rich, I would have it made." Feast mentality people give money a mystical power that it does not have. They see it as a hero who could rescue them from their mundane lives. Money can and will do no such thing. Instead money magnifies the inherent issues that exist.

Before Pam Doe[*] won an $87 million Powerball jackpot she thought, *if you've won the lotto, all your problems are over*. After her huge win, Pam was surprised to find that big money brings big money problems. On the nationally televised August 30, 1999, Oprah Winfrey Show, Pam admitted that "money only enhances who you really are." It may well enhance who your friends and family really are, too.

Nonetheless many, including Christians, throw their money away on pipe dreams. The lottery is the most popular gimmick around, especially in poor inner-city neighborhoods. Although the odds of winning are extremely remote, people empty their pockets daily in hope to select those winning numbers and are totally oblivious to the drawbacks.

State lotteries have gained so much momentum among Christians that Dale Vitalis developed the **Lord's Lottery:**

A Sure Fire Stewardship Program[3]

Theological Basis: 'As a man winneth so will he giveth.' (Hez 6:15)[4]

Purpose: The 'BLT' (bottom line theory) is to get more money to find its way into the offering plates on Sunday mornings.

---

[*] Pseudonym

[3] Circulated via internet in 1999

[4] No biblical reference. This is a joke.

Plan: Three simple steps to explosive giving:

1. When the ushers bring the offering plates to the altar the pastor will place all the offering envelopes in a big round tumbler on the altar.

2. One of the acolytes will step forward and draw out one of the offering envelopes from the big round tumbler on the altar.

3. The 'winner' (person or family whose offering envelope is drawn) will receive **DOUBLE THEIR MONEY BACK!!**

Benefits: Fee-nominal!! Listed below are some of the outstanding benefit blessings, if you serve a 'spiritual' congregation from this **'Lord's Lottery Sure Fire Stewardship Program'**

1. More and more members will begin using offering envelopes.

2. When you make the offering envelopes available only to members you will be astounded at how your membership will grow.

3. Members will naturally put in more money because they know that if their envelope is drawn they will get more back (never underestimate the intelligence of your members).

4. Your worship service will reach new heights of excitement. You can imagine the excitement and

drama each Sunday as the winning envelope is drawn.

5. You will have no trouble lining up acolytes because of the excitement, honor, and prestige that comes with the job.

6. Your finance committee will never again have to worry about buying those expensive offering envelope boxes. When this new program catches on members will be more than willing to buy their own. You will also discover that many will buy more than one set of envelopes. I call this the 'bingo syndrome.'

7. Pastors will no longer have to work quite so hard on their sermons as they will no longer be the 'main event.'

Obviously the Lord's Lottery is a witty jest, not intended to be taken seriously. There is no humor, however, in Christians demonstrating more faith in the lottery than they do in God.

A large percentage of people who inherit wealth are clueless about what they should do with it. "Attaining wealth proves to be a hollow achievement for many" says Jessie O'Neill, wealth counselor and author of the *Golden Ghetto: The Psychology of Affluence*. Jessie O'Neill is the granddaughter of Charles Erwin Wilson, one-time president of General Motors. She personally experienced "sudden wealth syndrome" when she inherited millions at 28 years old. Ms. O'Neill addresses issues which the newly rich experience. She found that "It is a peculiarly American notion that money will guarantee happiness, bring us personal fulfillment, strengthen our relationships, give us smarter, better-adjusted children -- in short, make all our dreams come true."[5] Most are devastated when they find out that this is false.

I would be remiss if I neglect to yield some consideration to the other extreme money misconception, the famine mentality. Opposite the feast mentality we find the famine mentality. Because it is as dangerous, volatile and destructive as its excessive counterpart, the famine mentality definitely deserves equal attention.

Have you ever been extremely hungry? Famished? At that point you are not thinking about what you would like to eat. It makes no difference if someone places your favorite dish in front of you or hands you a loaf of dry bread. If it is edible, you will eat it.

One can see this degree of hunger in pictures of children from third world countries. People who live in these distressed regions are literally starving. Just a glimpse at their malnourished bodies would cause you to lose your appetite for at least a week. When we witness people dying because they do not have necessities like food, clothing and shelter, we begin to better appreciate our blessings. "*The Lord will not allow the righteous soul to famish" (Proverbs 10:3)*

Unfortunately many of us do not realize there are people starving and in grave need in our own neighborhoods. Every major American metropolis has a skid row. Homelessness has become an issue of increasing concern for our nation. Today, we cannot drive down a city street without seeing indigence. Sadly many of us have become so accustomed to this we are no longer fazed by it. "*The destruction of the poor is their poverty" (Proverbs 10:15b).*

Webster's defines *famine* as extreme scarcity, great shortage, suffering for lack of a necessity and severe starvation. There is a famine in our land, and we seem to be doing very little about it.

---

[5] O'Neill, Jessie *The Golden Ghetto: The Psychology of Affluence*

I do not believe anyone of sound mind would choose poverty over abundant living. However, most of us live far beneath this God-given privilege. The famine mentality is largely responsible for this.

Scavengers Settle

In Leviticus 11, God prescribed a special diet to Israel, His chosen people. He forbade them to eat the meat of any unclean animal. Among the unclean animals He listed were pigs, snakes, rats, lizards, insects and aquatic scavengers such as shrimp, clams, oysters, and frogs. Not only did God command Israel to abstain from consuming these types of animals, He deplored their touching such animals. God said one who carries even the dead carcass of such an animal is unclean, and must wash his clothes, for a period (Leviticus 11:28).[6]

Although most of us would not dream of eating some of these animals, we were blessed and released to eat what we like. In the New Testament book of Acts, God gave Peter a vision. "*In it were all kinds of four-footed animals of the earth, wild beasts, creeping things, and birds of the air. And a voice came to him, 'Rise, Peter; kill and eat.'*"

But Peter said, "Not so Lord! For I have never eaten anything common or unclean."

And the voice spoke to him again the second time, "What God has cleansed you must not call common" (Acts 10:12-15).

Thus, the confinement and restraint of the law no longer exists because God's grace abounds to us, "*For you are not under law but under grace" (Romans 6:14b).*

---

[6] Paraphrased Leviticus Chapter 11

I do not criticize anyone's diet. I am originally from New Orleans, Louisiana and I have eaten my share of crawfish and other unclean animals. I occasionally still enjoy some of these 'suspect' foods. So I am the last person to judge what someone else decides to eat.

A lesson can be learned, however, from this special diet God gave Israel. He called these types of animals unclean because they are last on the totem poll. They are scavengers.

Webster's defines *scavenge*, to feed on dirt, refuse or discarded material. A scavenger is a junk man, a garbage collector, one whose livelihood requires him to remove dirt and refuse. Scavenger animals sink to the bottom of their domain and feed off of the remains which other animals leave behind.

I do not want to disgust you but I must be honest. You will find rodents consuming the garbage from your local dumpsite. Crabs, shrimp and other shellfish devour the remains and garbage which other marine life leave behind. Thus, scavengers settle for less and are satisfied with just that.

This scavenger illustration accurately portrays the famine mentality. God did not want us to eat unclean animals because He loves us. He felt that His chosen people deserved much better than the bottom of the food chain. Scavengers carry diseases and plagues as a result of the garbage they eat. They could bring our bodies more harm than any nutritional value we derive from them.

Again, we are now under grace. God has given us free will to choose and eat what we like. My grandmother used to tell me, "You are what you eat." Famine mentality individuals are like scavengers because they settle for less than God's will for them.

We reside in Los Angeles county. We know of a family that has lived in Los Angeles for more than fifty years, the

Smiths.[*] Derrick W. Hutchins wrote about such a family when he wrote an article in Ministries Today magazine's September 1997 issue on 21st Century Ministry, entitled, "Can We Save The Family?" He wrote,

> It's Saturday afternoon, and Lisa strolls through the mall in her urban neighborhood. Moving toward her is a muscular man pushing a shopping cart, his wife and children walking alongside him. Lisa knows that in some neighborhoods, such a scene would appear normal. But in her community, this couple represents one of the few intact families in the mall. All too common is the next group rounding the corner just ahead: five young women, each one pushing a baby stroller--and not one of them married.
>
> "Where are the men?" Lisa asks herself in frustration. It's a good question. Like her mother before her and her daughter after, Lisa had a child out of wedlock at 16. When her mother got pregnant in the 1950's, she was considered promiscuous. When Lisa had a baby in 1970, few ostracized her. By the time her own daughter had a baby, however, motherhood without marriage seemed almost normal. Today it's all too common.[7]

There are four generations of the Smith family in one household, soon to be five because the youngest is six months pregnant. Each generation has been on welfare her entire life. Unbelievably, none of the Smiths have ever gone to the beach.

---

[*] Pseudonym

[7] Huchins, Derrick W.
1997 Ministries Today: 21st-Century Ministry: page 67.

They live so close but have never taken advantage of a wonderful experience that is absolutely free.

The famine mentality perpetuates a scarcity philosophy. A person with this mind-set believes that there is only a limited amount of good to go around. As a result, he hoards his possessions because he fears not having enough in his time of need. The famine mentality individual will try to convince you that the earth has almost been depleted of all its natural resources. So, in order for you to have more, someone else must suffer loss. The truth is God provided us with everything we would ever need when He created the world. *"See, I have given you every herb that yields seed which is on the face of all the earth, and every tree whose fruit yields seed; to you it shall be for food" (Genesis 1:29).*

The famine mentality individual will become competitive, possessive, territorial and defensive if he feels threatened. This individual's primary objective is to maintain the status quo. Someone who asserts change can rest assured that he is in for the fight of his life. All scavengers can become vicious creatures when provoked.

However, the most troubling aspect of the famine mentality is the fact that the effects of it sneak up on you without notice. For example, it is fairly easy to remain within your comfort zone and never realize that valuable opportunities are passing you by. If you place a number of crabs in a barrel, they will try to climb out. The crabs that are not climbing will pull the climbers down before they are able to escape. We do not know why crabs are motivated to do this. Could the crabs have a malicious intent for their actions? Perhaps one crab pulls a fellow crab down in order to use it as a step to aid its own climb. Maybe the crabs simply want their group to remain together, like a family? Wandering off into foreign territory could prove to be very dangerous. It could possibly be better for the group to stay together, even die together, rather than have just one escape. Crabs are scavengers. They settle for less and are satisfied with just that.

Here is another way the famine mentality sneaks up without warning. If you drop a frog in boiling hot water, it will instantly leap out. Its survival instinct will bring it to safety. But place that same frog in a pot of cool water on the stove over a very low flame, and there it will remain and cook until it dies. The frog will not even perceive danger. Remember, frogs are also scavengers. They settle for less and are satisfied with just that.

Many Christians fall prey to a famine mentality. I have attended more storefront churches than I care to mention, where I have repeatedly heard I Timothy 6:10 misquoted by the minister. 'Money is the root of all evil' he says. And continues his declaration with, "Blessed are the poor..."

This happens frequently in the pulpits of poverty stricken neighborhoods across the country. It's no wonder that members of congregations in the most desolate communities are content living in poverty. They say, 'great will be our reward in heaven.' It is relatively easy to become *so heavenly minded that you are of no earthly good.*

I am very grateful for John 14:2 where we read Christ's promises, *"In my Father's house are many mansions; if it were not so, I would have told you. I go to prepare a place for you."* I have no doubt that heaven is awesome, for lack of a better term. I Corinthians 2:9 affirms *"Eye has not seen, nor ear hear heard, Nor have entered into the heart of man the things which God has prepared for those who love Him."*

We are not supposed to live the life of a scavenger. We are not to settle for less than God's best. He chose us. Ephesians 1:5,6 tells us that God adopted us as sons according to His good pleasure.[8] Romans 8:16,17 affirms, *"The Spirit*

[8] Paraphrase Ephesians 1:5,6

Himself bears witness with our spirit that we are children of God, and if children, then heirs -- heirs of God and joint heirs with Christ."

We were created for a purpose and there is a mission we should accomplish while here on earth. Jesus said, *"All authority has been given to Me in heaven and on earth. Go therefore and make disciples of all the nations, baptizing them in the name of the Father and of the Son and of the Holy Spirit, teaching them to observe all things that I have commanded you; and lo, I am with you always, even to the end of the age"* (Matthew 28:18, 19)

How far can we go to witness and proclaim the gospel without money? Most of us cannot afford to visit other countries or other states within this country. Sadly, some of us cannot travel to the end of our own residential block, because our lives do not illustrate God's glory. Instead, they display suffering, famine and lack. Could you effectively win anyone to Christ? If a sinner sees that she is living considerably better than you are, how will you ever convince her that Christ came so we might have life more abundantly.[9]

Any doctrine which states that Christians should live poor, meager lives is pious and unsupported by scripture. "*Riches and honor are with me, Enduring riches and righteousness" (Proverbs 8:18).*

I Timothy 6:10 actually reads, "*For the love of money is the root of all evil."* We are not supposed to love money. We are supposed to love God. He is the supplier of all our need according to his riches in glory by Christ Jesus.[10] Money is needed to accomplish the mission God gave us.

It is selfish to want just enough resources to make provision for yourself or your family. As Christians, we are blessed to be a blessing to others. If you do not have enough

[9] Paraphrased John 10:10
[10] Paraphrased Philippians 4:19

to spare, you simply do not have enough. A superior animal leaves his remains behind for the inferior scavenger. Famine mentality individuals are the scavengers that do not have leftovers.

Attitude of Altitude

So which do you choose, feast or famine? The right answer is neither. The best choice is the attitude of altitude. In Philippians 4:11,12 Apostle Paul genuinely expresses the true attitude of altitude when he says, *"I have learned in whatever state I am, to be content: I know how to be abased and know how to abound. Everywhere and in all things I have learned both to be full and to be hungry, both to abound and to suffer need."*

Unfortunately, most people have not developed a healthy attitude toward money. Many do not use money wisely. In general, people do not properly manage their resources. The primary function of money is still a medium of exchange. It buys us more options and opportunities. Money is a tool. Like a hammer, if you do not know how to use it correctly you can and probably will severely injure yourself.

We must develop an attitude of altitude if we want to control our finances instead of having our financial circumstances control us. Bishop Charles Edward Blake, pastor of West Angeles Church of God In Christ, proclaimed, as he taught from the book of Esther, "Your attitude determines your altitude." Simple development of the proper attitude will increase your altitude. If you want to go higher (have more) address your misconceptions about wealth.

Dr. Creflo Dollar of World Changers Ministry in College Park, Georgia says, "Christian money is money with a mission." Deuteronomy 8:18 states, *"And you shall remember the Lord your God, for it is He who gives you power to get wealth,* ***that He may establish His covenant*** *which He swore to your fathers, as it is this day."* The attitude of altitude is crucial because it encourages us to develop the right relationship and the right motives with regard to money. We are paid to do a job. And that job is to establish God's covenant upon this entire earth.

A friend of ours had a license plate frame that inspired one of our seminars. His vanity tag read, 'Paying the cost to be the boss.' The attitude of altitude is practical and realistic. In this workshop, Prosperity Outpouring To The Saints International (POTTS, Intl.) teaches individuals to count the cost. We pose this question to people from all walks of life: "If God blessed you with $1,000,000 today, what would you do with it?"

Most people respond: "I'd quit my job, buy a bigger house, an expensive car and go on a dream vacation." The truth is $500,000 of that million goes to federal and state taxes. If you tithe, $100,000 goes to your church. You are left with approximately $500,000 or less. Instantly, you become a half millionaire.

That bigger house you bought will cost you more in property taxes. A $400,000 home in Los Angeles, California will cost you roughly $4,000 in property taxes annually. Hopefully, you paid for the car in full. Otherwise you are left with a monthly note and no job, not to mention automobile insurance. If you've managed to save a substantial amount of money after making your purchases, be informed that banks insure a maximum of $100,000. A savings higher than that amount requires that you develop an alternative plan to insure the excess.

Oprah Winfrey often tells her audience that she does not believe in luck. She defines luck as "preparation meeting opportunity." We are in total agreement with Oprah on this issue. We do not believe in luck! When an opportunity presents itself, one must be prepared to take full advantage of it. Otherwise, he will not be blessed.

God has the power to bless any of us with millions, even billions of dollars instantly. But, He won't give us anything we are not ready, willing and able to receive. He loves us too much to allow us to blow it. "*The blessing of the Lord makes one rich And He adds no sorrow with it" (Proverbs 10:22).* POTTS, Intl. helps individuals get ready, prepared and positioned to get blessed.

Ask yourself the question, "Can God trust me with riches?" Remember, you must first be *faithful over few things to become ruler over many.*[11]

Develop the attitude of altitude. Count the cost! "*For the turning away of the simple shall slay them, and the prosperity of fools shall destroy them" (Proverbs 1:32).*[12]

---

[11] Paraphrase Matthew 25:21 Parable of the Talents

[12] Proverbs 1:32 King James Version

Chapter 3

What People Do For Money

Then Judas Iscariot, one of the twelve, went to the chief priests to betray Him to them. And when they heard it, they were glad, and promised to give him money...Mark 14:10,11

Today we have an endless list of career choices available to us. The United States Dictionary of Occupational Titles (DOT) lists hundreds of thousands of jobs that Americans perform on a daily basis. Each decade adds countless new professions to the register.

The twentieth-century work environment experienced drastic changes. Corporate restructuring, down sizing, right sizing and reorganizations have changed the faces of age-old employment positions. No longer do we work for the same employer forty plus years. Most individuals now make more than one career choice in a lifetime.

The Prostitution Ring

Although many changes continue to present themselves in the work force, the oldest profession in the world still exists. Prostitution is against the law in most states, but we still find it running rampant here in America as well as other countries.

The prostitution system withstands the test of time because it satisfies some fundamental human objectives:

(1) Prostitution enables one to profit from his or her most basic, primal skills.

(2) Prostitution establishes a routine series of business functions that an individual may perform without emotional attachment.

(3) Organized prostitution offers safety benefits.

Ironically, prostitution laid the framework for many of the employment positions we fill today. Do the above three objectives fit your job description? Many of us answer this question with a resounding yes. What do you do for money? Could it be that today's work force essentially amounts to a morally acceptable prostitution ring?

Several years ago Hollywood released a blockbuster film entitled "Indecent Proposal." The leading man was a billionaire who met a man and his wife while they were vacationing in Las Vegas, Nevada. The billionaire was attracted to the married woman, so he offered the man a million dollars to allow him to sleep with his wife. Although the couple was initially appalled by this unthinkable proposition, they gradually began to ponder the possibilities a million dollars would buy them. After careful consideration and debate the couple accepted the billionaire's offer and sealed the agreement. As a result, the once-very-much-in-love couple's relationship and lives began to fall apart at the seams. The moral of the story is everything is negotiable.

It is relatively easy to label people like Benedict Arnold and Judas Iscariot as unscrupulous traitors. One betrayed his country and the other betrayed the Christ. It is not very easy, however, to acknowledge that we betray ourselves by selling out on a daily basis. For one million dollars this couple paid dearly. Ask yourself these questions, "What is my price?" "Is everything negotiable?" Once you are ready to give yourself an honest answer read on.

Prostitution enables one to profit from his or her most basic, primal skills. The average person would like to be paid well for performing tasks that do not require a formal education or technical training. Most of us want to collect a paycheck for being our wonderful selves. This is not necessarily characterized by laziness, but human nature in general. The desire for a challenging career escapes us. Many remain in a designated employment position because it is easy, familiar and non-threatening. Most people want to obtain a maximum benefit by making a minimal sacrifice. If someone offered to pay us to function as doctors or lawyers without the requisite training, we would graciously accept. Some have committed fraud by falsifying academic transcripts, diplomas and certificates, lying on resumes and embellishing credentials in order to obtain choice employment positions.

Prostitution establishes a routine series of business functions that an individual may perform without emotional attachment. This describes a high percentage of the jobs in America, including some consultant positions. Every morning we arrive at our employment location and begin performing repetitive tasks. We repeat this process so often it becomes second nature to us. Most times we are on autopilot, virtually unconscious between the hours of 8:00 A.M. and 5:00 P.M. Perhaps we were excited, nervous and full of anticipation when we began our employ. But months and years later, we have become completely detached from the work we do on a daily basis. Many employees are programmed similar to the computer systems they operate in their various office spaces.

Organized prostitution offers safety benefits. Many of us have viewed movies portraying vivid scenes where a pimp asserts his authority over a prostitute. The prostitute is victimized in many ways. The pimp is usually the person who first lured the individual into prostitution. Often times the pimp introduces the prostitute to illegal drugs, leading her down a road of addiction. The prostitute usually fears the pimp because of his abusive nature. Nevertheless, she stays with him because he promises to protect her from unruly Johns, the police and anyone else who threatens to harm her. The pimp also provides the prostitute with the drugs she now desperately craves. In return the prostitute gives her pimp the money she earned on the street, and he gives her just enough to keep her coming back again and again.

I'm sure this analogy sounds quite extreme to a middle-class suburbanite. But many people remain with their employers because of the medical or retirement benefits offered. Most people do not realize that their employer is willing to pay them $20 an hour to perform duties because the business often derives many times that amount in profit from the services they provide. At times our managers and supervisors become insensitive and borderline abusive. They want employees to produce above and beyond the call of duty. Yet we stay because we are convinced that we cannot survive without that paycheck our employers have gotten us addicted to. We like the security of knowing we will be paid on the first and the fifteenth. We have become accustomed to the goods and services that payroll check buys us. We are hooked. Addicted. We feel trapped. Similar to the prostitute, we do not see a way out.

Dollars and Sense

Although it's clear we need money to survive and God wants us to have money so that we can effectively spread the gospel, we should make wise choices about how we obtain money. Money is a resource. The end does not justify the means. Possessing dollars without acquiring the *sense* to go along with them can cause ruin. Those same dollars could be rendered useless. They could also bring ones demise. The scripture bears witness, "*The prosperity of fools shall destroy them.*"[1] In Matthew 27:3-5, Judas Iscariot returned the thirty pieces of silver he was paid by the chief priests and hung himself.[2]

The *sense* we refer to in the previous paragraph is education. Long ago a statesman announced, "Ignorance is bliss." In doing so he popularized the mind-set many have today. We call these people "senseless" because they believe, 'What they don't know won't hurt them.' Time and time again this notion has been proven wrong. What you don't know could kill you.

We present a marriage enhancement seminar entitled, "First Aid for Marital Blisters." Couples who have been married close to a year or more especially appreciate this presentation. They've experienced each other enough to understand that a honeymoon could end tragically if mates do not invest time and effort in learning how to nurture their relationship so that a marriage can take root, grow and blossom into 'Happily Ever After.' Otherwise marital bliss can become marital blisters, which explains Apostle Peter's exhortation to husbands and wives, "*Dwell with them according to knowledge...that your prayers may not be hindered.*"[3]

Ignorant bliss regarding money turns into blisters also. *Webster's* defines the verb *blister*: "to administer severe physical punishment especially by whipping, or to scorch." Thus, blistering is a painful experience. Choosing to live by the philosophy, 'Ignorance is bliss' inevitably yields blistering wounds. Those who make this bad decision eventually have the scars to prove that what they did not know hurt them

---

[1] Proverbs 1:32b King James Version
[2] Paraphrased Matthew 27:3-7
[3] Paraphrased I Peter 3:7

dearly. However, education serves as a helmet, a body wrap or knee pads to insulate us from injury.

Remember the old adage, 'Give a man a fish and he will eat for a day, but teach him how to fish and he will eat for a lifetime.' POTTS, Intl. teaches financial empowerment because individuals should educate themselves about money in order to reap the benefits that accompany wealth. Jesus Christ said, *"Follow me and I will make you fishers of men" (Matthew 4:19).*

Empowering education starts with a genuine desire to learn. A teachable person is open to mastering new concepts, strategies and adventures. "Men and women are wise in proportion, not to their experience, but to their capacity for experience." - George Bernard Shaw

Chapter 4

Got Money?

Do not wear yourself out to get rich;
have the wisdom to show restraint. Proverbs 23:4[1]

In the late 1990's, the dairy industry launched the catchy ad, 'got Milk?' Television commercials display super models and prize-winning athletes with a mustache of milk above their mouths. We are left with the assumption that milk made them great because, 'Milk does a body good.' Another commercial shows a man dying. He arrives at a place he thinks is heaven, because there are all sorts of cookies, cakes, candies and decadent desserts available to him. But once he begins eating, he realizes that he is not in heaven at all. Instead he is in hell, because he has no milk to wash down these treats. The dairy industry is trying to tell us that being without milk is a fate worst than death. The truth is no matter what a glass of milk does for the body, we can survive without it. However, our chances of survival are slim and none without money. "Got Money?"

Every possible method of obtaining money presents both benefits and drawbacks. In chapter two, we introduced the concept, 'Counting the Cost.' Here's how we start the process: Consider the fact that individuals acquire money in a variety of ways from a wide variety of sources. There are eight commonly used methods of obtaining money. We either earn, inherit, win, find, beg, borrow, steal or grow money.

---

[1] Proverbs 23:4, New International Version

Earn Money

The most conventional way to acquire money is to earn it. Although we perhaps startled many of you last chapter with our crass description of prostitution, there is absolutely nothing wrong with earning an honest living by working for someone else as long as it aligns with your God-given purpose. We advocate developing an entrepreneurial spirit. However, we understand that self-employment is not for everyone. Self-employment necessitates a unique discipline, initiative, tenacity, independence, resourcefulness, ingenuity, organizational skill, and planning which an outside employer may or may not require to fill an employment position.

Again, there is nothing wrong with working for others. There may be a problem, however, with our attitude regarding occupation. We tend to judge ourselves and others based on what we do for a living. For instance, whenever we meet strangers, one of the first questions we ask concerns the nature of their work. This may indicate more than personal interest or curiosity. When we learn about another person's work, we often are able to make assumptions about his or her education, social status, and economic level.[2] Ones income is determined largely by ones work. In turn, income can influence the person's lifestyle, place of residence, choice of friends, leisure activities, feelings of self worth, and general satisfaction with life. People who like their work are often happy with life in general. When a person is not happy at work, this unhappiness can permeate all of life.[3]

Sometimes the unhappiness comes near the start of one's career, but often it appears after several years. Some

---

[2] Collins, Gary R.
1988 *Christian Counseling: A Comprehensive Guide*: Dallas: Word Publishing: page 546.
[3] Ibid.

people move up corporate or professional ladders only to conclude that they are bored, burned out, tired of the stress, and wanting a new challenge.[4] Many wonder if they would be better suited, more satisfied, more successful, and a lot happier in some other occupation. People who feel euphoric on Friday afternoons and depressed on Sunday nights probably aren't happy in their careers, but for many thoughts of change go no further than restless dreaming. Few are willing to accept any new opportunities that may come along. Most people lack the considerable courage to seriously review career goals and, if necessary, to uproot themselves or their families and change vocational direction. It is easier to accept the current situation and make the best of it.[5]

March 27, 2000, Oprah Winfrey read a study done by the Wall Street Journal on her nationally televised show. "The study concluded that more than half of all working individuals would choose another line of work if they had the chance; which means that more than half of all working individuals are unhappy in their current jobs." Thus, the majority of our work force is displaced. Let's examine a few of the many factors that could cause one to make the wrong career choice.

High status, high prestige, and high-paying jobs are relatively scarce, but are sought by numerous people. Many of the more attractive professional and entertainment careers require intellectual abilities, unique aptitudes, specialized training, and sometimes personal contacts that few people possess.[6] Because of the high demand, intense competition,

---

[4] Collins, Gary R.
1988 *Christian Counseling: A Comprehensive Guide:* Dallas: Word Publishing: page 546.
[5] Berkeley Rice
1985 "Why Am I in This Job?" Psychology Today 19: page 54-59
[6] Collins, Gary R.
1988 *Christian Counseling: A Comprehensive Guide*: Dallas: Word Publishing: page 543.

and limited opportunities, many people are disappointed in their career choices and forced to settle for less desirable alternatives.[7]

Others never have the opportunity to plan careers. In need of work, these people skim the classified section of the newspaper and slip into jobs that provide a paycheck and some security but are neither satisfying nor personally fulfilling. Some people stay in these jobs for their entire lives. They often are part of the 50 to 80 percent of the work force that is in the wrong type of work.[8] Most of these people are dissatisfied and unhappy. Some get laid off or shift from one position to another, none of which they enjoy or do well.[9]

Even people who enjoy their work often make changes as they go through life. Government estimates suggest that ten years from now nearly half of the working population will be in jobs that have not yet been developed. Young people who are entering the work force can expect to change jobs twelve to fifteen times during their working lives, and most will change careers four or five times.[10]

There was a time when choosing a career was seen as a once in a lifetime event that occurred in late adolescence or early adulthood. Little children were prepared for this ominous choice whenever they were asked, "What will you be when you grow up?" College students were forced to make an early

---

[7] Collins, Gary R.
1988 *Christian Counseling: A Comprehensive Guide:* Dallas: Word Publishing: page 543.
[8] Mattson, Ralph and Miller, Arthur
1982 *Finding A Job You Can Love*: Nashville: Thomas Nelson
[9] Collins, Gary R.
1988 *Christian Counseling: A Comprehensive Guide*: Dallas: Word Publishing: page 543
[10] Haldane, Bernard and Jean and Martin, Lowell
1976 *Job Power Now! The Young Peoples Job Finding Guide*: Washington DC: Acropolis Books

choice of their majors and often it was assumed, especially by parents, that the primary purpose of education was to prepare students for successful careers and the making of wise vocational choices. Hence, well-meaning and concerned parents pushed their sons and daughters to decide what to do with their lives.[11]

We are still presented with both family and social influences today. In our society, teachers, friends, relatives and especially parents tend to expect that career decisions will be made early.[12] At a time when young people are immature, idealistic, inexperienced, and struggling with the problems of late adolescence, they have the added responsibility of choosing from an almost unlimited number of career possibilities. Later in life, if one quits or is forced to leave a job there is financial and social pressure to find other work as quickly as possible. All of this prevents careful planning and encourages vocational choices that can lead to disappointment and frustration.[13]

Because career choice and degree of success can touch and influence almost every other area of life, including the spiritual, we should consider factors that increase our odds of making good vocational decisions. A well thought-out career

---

[11] Collins, Gary R.
1988 *Christian Counseling: A Comprehensive Guide*: Dallas: Word Publishing: page 539

[12] Davis, M. and Kandell, D.B.
1981 "Parental and Peer Influences on Adolescents' Educational Plans: Some Further Evidence," American Journal of Sociology 87: pp. 363-387
Lopez, Frederick G. and Andrews, Scott and Okiishi, Rae Wieners
1987 "Career Indecision: A Family Systems Perspective: The Genogram as a Tool in Career Counseling," Journal of Counseling and Development 65 and 66: pages 304-307 and pages 139-143

[13] Collins, Gary R.
1988 *Christian Counseling: A Comprehensive Guide*: Dallas: Word Publishing: page 543

plan should include personality influences, interests, aptitudes or abilities.

An individual's personality affects both the selection of a vocation and the success or satisfaction that is experienced within one's career. One writer suggested that most people can be categorized into six general vocational personality types: realistic (the person who prefers tangible, practical, skill activities), investigative (the one who is methodical, intellectual, curious, and scientific), artistic (the creative, aesthetically oriented person) social (he or she who is friendly, sensitive, and interested in people), enterprising (the aggressive, energetic, self-confident problem solver), and conventional (the person who prefers routine and orderly, practical, somewhat inflexible activities).[14] It's never possible to fit people into rigid categories. The theory does suggest that most people have a dominant personality type, which emerges between the ages of eighteen and thirty, plus one or two less prominent types. These individual differences bear on career choice, satisfaction and success.[15]

According to the same theory, jobs also can be divided into six categories: realistic, investigative, artistic, social, enterprising, and conventional. If investigative people enter investigative work (such as scientific research) or if artistic people enter artistic occupations (like writing, painting, or acting), there will be a high degree of satisfaction. In contrast, if a socially inclined person gets into a realistic type of job, or

---

[14] Holland, John I.
1985 *Making Vocational Choices: A Theory of Vocational Personalities and Work Environments*: New Jersey: Prentice-Hall
[15] Collins, Gary R.
1988 *Christian Counseling: A Comprehensive Guide*: Dallas: Word Publishing: page 543

if an enterprising person enters a conventional occupation, there is certain to be frustration and unhappiness.[16]

Another assumption is people will do best in those activities and occupations that interest them most. If a job is boring, it's unlikely to bring much personal fulfillment or satisfaction, even if the salary is high.[17]

Why do people choose vocations for which they have no interest? Sometimes in their need and desire to find employment, people take whatever job is available whether or not they find it interesting. Often these people expect to change positions later, but frequently, because of insufficient training or lack of opportunities, they do not or cannot change. Others take a boring job because of the salary or fringe benefits. It appears that many of the least desirable jobs in our society have a high level of remuneration in order to attract and retain workers. Since many of these workers have little interest in their work, they look for fulfillment and satisfaction in leisure-time activities, including sports, social clubs, church work, or sometimes drinking.[18]

A commercial airline has as part of its slogan, "doing what we do best!" When we have jobs that involve "doing what we do best," there often is high vocational fulfillment, good work efficiency, and low rates of absenteeism and turnover. In contrast, workers feel frustrated and are poorer employees when they are unable to do what the job requires or

---

[16] Collin, Gary R.
1988 *Christian Counseling: A Comprehensive Guide*: Dallas: Word Publishing: page 544
[17] Hansen, Jo-Ida C.
1987 E. K. Strong, Jr., "First Author of the Strong Interest Inventory," Journal of Counseling and Development 66: page 119
[18] Collins, Gary R.
1988 *Christian Counseling: A Comprehensive Guide*: Dallas: Word Publishing: page 544

when their work gives little opportunity for achieving one's greatest potential.[19]

Technically there is a difference between aptitude and ability. Aptitude refers to the potential that one has for learning something in the future. Ability refers to skills that one has at present or other learning that has taken place in the past. A young student, for example, may have an aptitude (good potential and capacity) for learning music, but it is only after years of study and practice that he or she may demonstrate great ability (skill and knowledge) as a musician.[20]

Careers are most satisfying when one's aptitudes and abilities relate to one's work. It has been estimated, however, that perhaps 80 percent of working people are underemployed; that is, working below their capacity and ability levels.[21] This is especially difficult for people who are gifted and unusually talented but forced to work in occupations where their skills and capabilities are not needed and rarely used.[22] Even highly intelligent people experience this frustration, because they consider underemployment to be better than unemployment. As a result some spent their whole working lives feeling unhappy, unfulfilled, and dissatisfied with their work.[23] We can

---

[19] Collins, Gary R.
1988 *Christian Counseling: A Comprehensive Guide:* Dallas: Word Publishing: page 544
[20] Ibid.
[21] Bolles, R.N.
1986 *What Color Is Your Parachute? A Practical Manual for Job Hunters and Career Changers*: Berkeley: Ten Speed Press
[22] Fredrickson, Ronald H.
1986 "Preparing Gifted and Talented Children for the World of Work," Journal of Counseling and Development 64:pp.556 and 557
[23] Collins, Gary R.
1988 *Christian Counseling: A Comprehensive Guide*: Dallas: Word Publishing: page 544.

safely conclude that vocational choices are crucially important, frequently difficult, and rarely once-in-a lifetime events.

* They are important because one's income, standard of living, status in the community, social contacts, emotional well-being, feelings of self-worth, use of time, and general satisfaction with life.

* They are difficult because of the many available careers, the staggering array of jobs, the great potential of making mistakes, and the misery that can come when we get into the wrong line of work.[24] According to a 1987 report by the Chicago Tribune, 24.3 percent of American workers are unhappy because they chose the wrong occupation or profession, one-third of middle managers wish they could work some place else, and about half of all employees feel they are underpaid.[25]

* Career choices are rarely once-in-a-lifetime events, because most people learn through experience.[26] Beginning in high school or even before, people start making decisions about work. The decisions continue as educational courses, college majors, and further training are all considered.[27] Vocational decisions also

---

[24] Collins, Gary R.
1988 *Christian Counseling: A Comprehensive Guide*: Dallas: Word Publishing: page 540.
[25] Kleiman, Carol
1987 "Hate Your Job? Welcome to the Club" Chicago Tribune 18
[26] Dillard, John Milton
1985 *Lifelong Career Planning*: Columbus, Ohio: Merrill
[27] Collins, Gary R.
1988 *Christian Counseling: A comprehensive Guide*: Dallas: Word Publishing: page 540.

> come whenever one applies for a job, is offered a position, is promoted, changes work, is fired or laid off, reevaluates a career, or faces retirement. For the Christian, all of these are influenced by the belief that one's vocational choices should be in accordance with God's will.[28]

After briefly examining what work is and what it represents to us, let's now take a look at what work should be, what work was intended to be. Work is God-ordained. It is part of his original intention for human beings. Work however, no longer is the pure joy that God intended it to be. Sin has caused work to become a burden,[29] especially when rich employers hoard their wealth and exploit their underpaid workers.[30] Some make work an idol and drive themselves in the vain accumulation of wealth and achievements.[31] Others pour their skills and efforts into work and anxious striving, only to wonder if all of their efforts are useless and without meaning.[32]

Adam was given the job of naming all living creatures and was instructed to subdue the earth and rule over it. After the original sin, Adam along with Eve, was banished from the Garden or Eden. Adam was sentenced to work the ground through painful toil and by the sweat of his brow.[33]

Throughout the Bible other examples of work appear frequently. Cain, the first child of Adam and Eve, cultivated the soil, and his brother Abel kept flocks. For at least part of

---

[28] Collins, Gary R.
1988 *Christian Counseling: A Comprehensive Guide:* Dallas: Word Pubishing: page 540

[29] Genesis 3:17-19

[30] James 5:3-5

[31] Ecclesiastes 2:4-11

[32] Ecclesiastes 2:17-23

[33] Genesis 3:17, 19,23

his life Noah was a shipbuilder. Later he turned to farming. Abraham was a wealthy livestock owner. David was a shepherd who later changed careers and became a king. Prophets, priests, tent makers, hunters, political leaders, sales persons, homemakers, real estate dealers, carpenters, fishermen, all of these and more are mentioned in the Bible as occupations for both men and women. It appears, therefore, that work has always been part of God's plan for the human race. After the fall work became harder, but it has always been God-ordained and a human responsibility.[34]

God has given work a new dignity and made it a source of blessing. Work is to be as a service to Christ. We do our jobs, not primarily to please our employers, "but with sincerity of heart and reverence for the Lord. Whatever you do, work at it with all your heart, as working for the Lord, not for men." According to Colossians, it is the Lord Christ we are serving,[35] even when we work for a non-Christian employer.
Work brings glory to God, helps others and brings personal benefits. Although God is our source, in order to eat, most of us have to work.[36] Regrettably many Christians have lost the biblical perspective on work and have accepted secular thinking about vocations.[37]

Work, like every other method of obtaining money, presents both benefits and drawbacks. The most profound benefits of earning money are societal impact and work ethic. Christians should be concerned about making a positive impact on society. Fulfillment is taking pleasure in the contribution

---

[34] Collins, Gary R.
1988 *Christian Counseling: A Comprehensive Guide*: Dallas: Word Publishing: page 541.
[35] Colossians 3:22-24
[36] 2 Thessalonians 3:10-12
[37] Collins, Gary R.
1988 *Christian Counseling: A Comprehensive Guide:* Dallas: Word Publishing: page 540.

that our work is making to the community. If we view decisions about our career only through the lens of self-satisfaction or self-interest, we are not being biblical people. Disciples of Jesus Christ must view career decisions not simply through the lens of self-gratification but through the lens of the needs of God's people - indeed, of human needs whenever they are found.[38]

Work is for the common good. The Bible points out that we each have unique capabilities and responsibilities.[39] When a person becomes a Christian, he or she is given one or more spiritual gifts. These are to be developed, used for the common good, and applied to the building up of other believers in the Body of Christ.[40] Our differences in abilities come from God, and it is he who allows some to become visibly successful. Because of this, the Christian has no reason for self-centered boasting about his or her accomplishments.[41]

What is most important in life? Succeeding generations tend to answer this question in different ways, but one study found that three values influence the career choices of many college students: helping people, having the opportunity to be creative, and succeeding in terms of money or status[42] (not necessarily in that order). Others want to change society, attain independence, find the best working conditions, or have the greatest possible influence for Christ.

Values can be important in career choice and career satisfaction or dissatisfaction. The worker who values honesty,

---

[38] Bernbaum and Steer, *Why Work?* 4.

[39] Collins, Gary R.
1988 *Christian Counseling: A Comprehensive Guide*: Dallas: Word Publishing: page 543

[40] Romans 12:3-8; I Corinthians 12:4-31; Ephesians 4:7-13

[41] Romans 12:3; Jeremiah 9:23,24

[42] Osipow, S. H.
1973 Theories of Career Development, 2nd ed. East Norwalk, Conn.: Appleton-Century-Crofts

for example, works best for an employer who is also honest. The same worker likely will be intensely frustrated if he or she is employed by a company where dishonesty and shady business deals are common.[43]

Another benefit of earning money is the fact that it establishes a good work ethic. The book of Proverbs repeatedly exhorts us to diligence. For example: Proverbs 10:4 says, "*He who has a slack hand becomes poor, but the hand of the diligent makes rich.*" Proverbs 12:24 says, "*The hand of the diligent will rule, but the lazy man will be put to forced labor.*" Proverbs 12:27 says, "*The lazy man does not roast what he took in hunting, but diligence is a man's precious possession.*" Proverbs 13:4 says "*The soul of a lazy man desires, and has nothing; but the soul of the diligent shall be made rich.*"

Clearly work is to be of high quality. Employees and other workers have a responsibility to work honestly and diligently,[44] not merely to please others, but to honor Christ. The pursuit of excellence is a worthy goal; dishonest and shoddy workmanship are unbiblical.[45] Employers are to be fair and just, recognizing that they too have a master in heaven.[46] Each of us must develop and show good stewardship of the talents and aptitudes that God has given.[47] The Christian's work is to be characterized by sincerity, enthusiasm, diligence, devotion to Christ, good will, discipline,

---

[43] Collins, Gary R.
1988 *Christian Counseling: A Comprehensive Guide*: Dallas: Word Publishing: page 544
[44] Ecclesiasties 9:10
[45] Engstrom, Ted W.
1982 *The Pursuit of Excellence*: Grand Rapids, Michigan: Zondervan
[46] Ephesians 6:5-9; Colossians 3:22, 4:1
[47] Matthew 25:14-30; Romans 12:6-8

quietness, cooperation, honesty, integrity, generosity, gratitude and efficiency.[48]

Earning money also presents some drawbacks. Earning money expends time and energy and it requires labor. Though redeemed from the curse, work still is not necessarily easy. For many of us, full time employment takes up 8, 9, sometimes even 10-12 hours of our day; time we would much rather spend with our families, on hobbies we enjoy or simply relaxing. Work can be a source of sleep deprivation, stress, unhealthy eating habits and failing relationships. Adverse work conditions may sap our energy, enthusiasm and creativity. Yet a large percentage of individuals explore no options other than work for financial support.

Work is by far the most popular method of obtaining money. It includes selling our material goods as well as our services. For many of us, work is like breathing. No matter what it entails, we cannot survive without it. Because work is such a major aspect of our lives, it should be chosen wisely and guided by God. We should not take lightly the way we earn money.

---

[48] Friesen, Gary
1980 *Decision Making and the Will of God*: Portland Oregon: Multnomah page 337 and based on Ephesians 6:5-7; Colossians 3:17

Chapter 5

Living on Purpose

And we know that all things work together for good to those who love God, to those who are the called according to His purpose.
Romans 8:28

There are eight methods of obtaining money. In the last chapter we discussed earning money, the most conventional approach. The next five chapters will examine the remaining seven methods; inheriting money, winning money, finding money, begging for money, borrowing money, stealing money and growing money.

At this juncture, it would be inappropriate to close the subject of earning money without explaining the concept of "purpose." Everyone born into this world was created for a purpose, a divine purpose. Psalm 139:13-16 says, "*For You formed my inward parts; You covered me in my mother's womb. I will praise You, for I am fearfully and wonderfully made. Marvelous are Your works, and that my soul knows well. My frame was not hidden from You, when I was made in secret, and skillfully wrought in the lowest parts of the earth. Your eyes saw my substance, being yet unformed. And in your book they all were written, the days fashioned for me, when as yet there were none of them.*"

Unfortunately, today many individuals are unhappy and unfulfilled in their jobs. This brings us to the conclusion that most people are merely existing, not living on purpose at all. It also explains why there is a mass of current information about people pursuing their passion.

Both work and vocational choice should be guided by God. The Bible shows us clear examples of people whose life's work was selected by God before their birth; Isaiah, Jeremiah, John the Baptist and Jesus are just a few.[1]

Most Christians would agree that God still chooses men and women to accomplish special tasks for him. However, many Christians question whether or not God has one specific career calling for each of his children. We know that he directs those who acknowledge him and seek his ways,[2] and we can be sure that he gives wisdom to those who ask.[3] Yet Christian workers question, "What role does my effort play, and what role does God play?" The answer lies in the Bible. Philippians 2:13 says, "*It is God who works in you both to will and to do for His good pleasure.*" God works in us through the Holy Spirit but we must submit and act in obedience. Thus, the prosperous, successful worker makes the dual assumption:

* My future is in God's hands and guided by his Holy Spirit.

* I have in my own hands the stewardship responsibility for developing my own talents, aptitudes, and abilities.[4]

Surely we can see work as "something to which God calls us and something he can use to give divine order to our lives.[5] Psalm 37:23 says, "*The steps of a good man are ordered by the Lord, and He delights in his way.*"

---

[1] Isaiah 49:1,5; Psalm 139:13-16; Jeremiah 1:5; Luke 1:13-17, 30-33
[2] Proverbs 3:5,6; Psalm 32:8
[3] James 1:5; Romans 12:1,2
[4] Slocum, Robert E.
1986 *Ordinary Christians in a High-Tech World*: Waco, Texas: Word Publishing: pages 162 and 163
[5] Ibid. pages 155-156; See also
Sherman, Doug and Hendricks, William
1988 *Your Work Matters to God*: Colorado Springs: NavPress

Motivational Gifts

God the Father, creator of the universe and all things, gave each of us a purpose. He also gave us spiritual gifts. God gave us life.[6] We are here solely because of Him.[7] He weaved gifts, talents and abilities in us as he formed us in our mother's womb.[8] The motivational gifts, listed in Romans 12:3-8, point us to our basic life purpose. The motivational gifts of God the Father should not be confused with the manifestational gifts of the Holy Spirit listed in 1Corinthians 12:8-10 or the five-fold ministry gifts of the Son listed in Ephesians 4:11. These gifts of God the Father lay the foundation of our basic "motivations," that is, inherent tendencies that characterize each different person by reason of the Creator's unique workmanship in their initial gifting.[9]

Remember Jesus gave us all the same mission, *"Go therefore and make disciples of all nations, baptizing them in the name of the Father and of the Son and of the Holy Spirit, teaching them to observe all things that I have commanded you; and lo, I am with you always, even to the end of the age" (Matthew 28:19,20).* This is frequently referred to as the Great Commission. It calls all Christians to take an active role in spreading the gospel.

Mission and purpose are not identical. One's purpose is as unique to that individual as his or her fingerprint. Your purpose facilitates your mission. When you operate in your purpose, you accomplish the Great Commission.

---

[6] Genesis 2:7

[7] Hebrews 12:9

[8] Psalm 139:13-16

[9] Walker, Paul Dr. Pastor, Mount Paran Church of God Atlanta, GA 1991 Spirit Filled Study Bible: Holy Spirit Gifts and Power: Nashville, TN: Thomas Nelson Inc. page 2023

Similarly, your motivational gifts direct you to your individual purpose. Motivation is the vehicle that transports you to your destination, i.e. purpose. Your gifts are not your purpose. Yet, you are motivated to act. Thus, understanding and developing your motivational gifts are prerequisite to living a purposeful life.

There are seven motivational giftings[10]:

1. **PROPHECY**
   a. To speak with forthrightness and insight, especially when enabled by the Spirit of God. *Joel 2:28*
   b. To demonstrate moral boldness and uncompromising commitment to worthy values.
   c. To influence others in one's arena of influence with a positive spirit of social or spiritual righteousness.

2. **MINISTRY**
   a. To minister and render loving, general service to meet the needs of others.
   b. Illustrated in the work and office of the deacon. *Matthew 20:26*

---

[10] Walker, Paul Dr. Pastor, Mount Paran Church of God Atlanta, GA 1991 Spirit Filled Study Bible: Holy Spirit Gifts and Power: Nashville, TN: Thomas Nelson Inc: page 2023

3. **TEACHING**
   a. The supernatural ability to explain and apply the truths received from God for the church.
   b. Presupposes study and the Spirit's illumination providing the ability to make divine truth clear to the people of God.
   c. Considered distinct from the work of the prophet who speaks as the direct mouth-piece of God.

4. **EXHORTATION**
   a. Literally means to call aside for the purpose of making an appeal.
   b. In a broader sense it means to entreat, comfort, or instruct. *Acts 4:36; Heb 10:25*

5. **GIVING**
   a. The essential meaning is to give out of a spirit of generosity.
   b. In a more technical sense it refers to those with resources aiding those without such resources. *2 Corinthians 8:2; 9:11-13*

6. **LEADERSHIP**
   a. Refers to the one "standing in front."
   b. Involves the exercise of the Holy Spirit in modeling, superintending, and developing the body of Christ.
   c. Leadership is to be exercised with diligence.

7. **MERCY**
   a. To feel sympathy with the misery of another.
   b. To relate to others in empathy, respect, and honesty.
   c. To be effective, this gift is to be exercised with kindness and cheerfulness - not as a matter of duty.

These gifts characterize our place in God's created order. They are foundational. Some may identify their motivational gifts from the aforementioned outline. However, observation indicates that few people are fully described by only one. More commonly a mix is found, with different traits of each gift present to some degree, while usually one will be the dominant trait of that person.[11]

There are many tests designed to help individuals identify their motivational gifts. We recommend the Team Ministry Spiritual Gifts Inventory designed by Dr. Larry Gilbert and published by the Church Growth Institute at P.O. Box 7000, Forest, VA 24551. The cost is a nominal fee of $2.50. This test is quite comprehensive and should relieve any doubt pertaining to one's motivational gifting.

Again, your motivational gifts of God the Father direct you to your purpose, that distinct task he placed you on this earth to complete. Motivation is the vehicle that transports you to your destination, i.e. purpose. For example: The prophet may drive a car to get to his destiny. The teacher may ride the bus. Perhaps the leader rides a motorcycle. The

---

[11] Walker, Paul Dr. Pastor Mount Paran Church of God Atlanta, GA 1991 Spirit Filled Study Bible: Holy Spirit Gifts and Power: Nashville, TN: Thomas Nelson Inc: page 2024

exhorter might take the subway. Get the point? Just as each person in the example took a different mode of transportation, motivational gifts are indicators of how people go about producing. This does not diminish the importance of getting the job done.

One might ask, "How do my motivational gifts relate to my daily life?" Frank Sinatra said it best with his popular hit, *I Did It My Way*. Wherever you choose to go and whatever you choose to do, your motivational gifts are always right there with you. These gifts are foundational. For instance, Dr. Martin Luther King, Jr. was a prophetic clergyman and civil rights leader. Mother Theresa was a giving nun. Thurgood Marshall was a teaching United States Supreme Court Justice. Eleanor Roosevelt was a leading first lady. Jimmy Carter was a merciful President of the United States. Maya Angelou is a ministering writer and poet. Sidney Portier is an exhorting actor.

Likewise, you might be a teaching politician, a leading secretary, a giving accountant or a prophetic engineer. Your gifts come as automatic to you as breathing. You do not even have to think about it. It helps to identify and develop your gifts. Naturally, an individual might be better suited for certain occupations. If your gifting drastically clashes with your chosen profession, life can become extremely difficult. Doing something that disagrees with who you are can bring misery and misery is contagious. Misery spreads like an epidemic, contaminating everyone who comes in contact.

Have you ever been a member of a club or organization where the president lacked the gift of leadership? Perhaps you have been a patient in a hospital or medical clinic where your nurse or attending physician did not possess the gift of mercy. Ingredients like these make a recipe for disaster. A negative experience is almost inevitable. These individuals are probably not living life on purpose.

Correct Career

Are you wondering if you chose the right job? Ask yourself this question: "Would I do what I do for free?" That is correct. A sure-fire method of identifying purpose in your life rests on your ability to be honest enough to admit whether or not you would still do what you do without being paid for it. On-purpose people pursue excellence in the absence of approval, prestige and money.

Too often we target careers in law, medicine or business because our parents, friends and teachers perceive these fields to be prominent and secure.* These jobs may buy us a house on a hill and a nice car along with various other material possessions and status symbols. However, a large percentage of us on this vocational track begin our professional careers by accumulating thousands of dollars of student loans from our law school, medical school or business school tuition.

No one bothered to tell us that most millionaires are self-employed and one out of five millionaires do not have a college degree.[12] Many times the costs of a misguided career choice outweigh the benefits. We pay dearly with our unhappiness, stress, long hours of work and dwindling self worth. This does not necessarily subtract from one's competence or quality of work. Possessing the talent, training or intellect to do a job does not presuppose purpose. In other words, the fact that I can do the work does not mean that I am the one for that particular job.

---

* Some people forge superficial relationships with perceivably prominent individuals because they believe such associations enhance their social status.

[12] Stanley, Thomas J. and Danko, William D. Ph.Ds
1996 The Millionaire Next Door: New York, NY: Pocket Books

Please understand that your level of income, possessions and social status do not define who you are. God, your creator does. *"For in Him we live and move and have our being" (Acts 17:28).* It is fine to have money and possessions, but they should not have you. Bishop Charles E. Blake, pastor of West Angeles Church of God in Christ of Los Angeles, California says, "I have never seen a U-Haul behind a hearse." Contrary to popular belief you cannot take anything with you.

The people you may try to impress probably want to impress you. Apostle Paul cautions us, *"I say then: Walk in the Spirit and you shall not fulfill the lust of the flesh. Now the works of the flesh are ...contentions, jealousies (emulations),...selfish ambitions,...envy,... those who practice such things will not inherit the kingdom of God" (Galatians 5:16-21).*[13] There is a modern day effort to 'keep up with the Joneses.' My question is: "Who are the Joneses anyway?"

Webster's defines *contention* as an act of contending through rivalry or competition; *jealousy* as zealous vigilance and hostility toward one believed to enjoy an advantage; *emulation* to strive to equal or excel others (as in achievement); and *envy* as malice or resentful awareness of an advantage enjoyed by another joined with a desire to possess the same advantage. The term *selfish ambition*, I believe, is self-explanatory.

Our quest should be desiring what God wants for us. Vain competitive thoughts and deeds lead us down the road of despair and hopelessness. There will always be someone smarter, faster, richer, prettier or taller. We cannot do anything about that, so what's the use! It is senseless to be jealous or envious of someone else's gift, opportunity or achievement. God has placed something very special in each and every one of his children. No other human being can

[13] Paraphrased Galatians 5:16-21

match you or replace you. If you resist the urge to 'keep up with the Joneses,' your quality of life will soar and you will soon realize that nobody but God himself can keep up with you. What you think about yourself is far more important than what anyone else may think of you. Be mindful of factors you allow to influence your life decisions. *"As a man thinks in his heart, so is he."*[14]

Purpose Unknown

Everyone alive today is here for a reason. You were born to do something special. Unfortunately, many of us are oblivious to our God-given purpose. Jesus said, *"For many are called, but the chosen are few" (Matthew 20:16).* It is not enough to have a particular calling on your life. You must answer the call to live on purpose. *"And we know that all things work together for good to those who love God, to those who are the called according to His purpose" (Romans 8:*28). How can people become fulfilled and experience true joy in their occupations or in their lives without realizing their purpose? It is impossible.

Remember we referred to the motivational gifts as vehicles. Well, imagine yourself walking out your door and getting into your car. You notice your neighbor doing the same. However, your neighbor knows exactly where she is going. But you are just driving around aimlessly.

Sometimes you end up in nice places. Often times you end up in not so nice places. Your biggest problem, however, is never knowing where you will end up. It would be helpful to at least have an idea of which direction is best. There is some comfort in knowing that you can always return home.

---

[14] Paraphrased Proverbs 23:7

Notwithstanding, you must continue the process again and again everyday.

This is precisely what it is like to have an unknown purpose. One is left wandering, wondering and wavering. A majority of people live life by chance, by accident, by coincidence and possibly even by predicament. In essence they are not living at all, merely existing. Certainly children of the Most High God deserve better.

Pursuing Purpose

How can one find his or her purpose? Apostle Paul provides us with a map, "*And we know that all things work together for good to those who love God, to those who are the called according to His purpose.*"[15]

You must love God. To know Him is to love Him. He is a friend who sticks closer than a brother.[16] One maintains a good relationship with his or her best friend. They talk everyday. The relationship is not self-serving or one-sided, but genuine. God wants this type of relationship with all of His children. David was a man after God's own heart.[17] He sought God in prayer and praised and worshipped God in song constantly. As a result, God made him king of Israel. When you spend quality time with God on a daily basis and seek His will for your life, He shall reveal your purpose. Sometimes the revelation is gradual and other times it is pronounced. The answer may come through an individual, in a dream or while reading the Bible.

Knowing is only half the battle. One must do more than just understand and acknowledge his or her purpose.

[15] Romans 8:28

[16] Paraphrased Proverbs 18:24

[17] Acts 13:22

Faith without works is dead.[18] One must live out that purpose. This may be easier said than done. It frequently requires moving beyond what is familiar and going outside your comfort zone. Although it is human nature to fear the unknown, blessings come with obedience. That's how God worked with Abram. *Now the Lord had said to Abram: "Get out of your country, from your family and from your father's house, to a land that I will show you. I will make you a great nation: I will bless you and make your name great; and you shall be a blessing. I will bless those who bless you and I will curse him who curses you; and in you all the families of the earth shall be blessed" (Genesis 12:1-3).*

In January 1994, I cried out to the Lord and He placed a calling on my life. I was lying in my bed diagnosed with chronic bronchitis when the Lord spoke to me as He did to Abram.

At that time, I was attending law school and already working at a prestigious law firm in New Orleans, Louisiana. Imagine my reaction when God told me, in no uncertain terms, to leave the only place I had ever called home. I immediately asked two questions. The first was, "Where do you want me to go?" And, the second was, "Why?" As promptly as I asked him, He answered me. He told me, "Go to Los Angeles, because I said so." I had just finished watching national media coverage of the devastating damage done by a Los Angeles earthquake which occurred earlier that morning.

Initially I thought the bronchitis had me delirious, but I could not ignore this command. I could not even sleep without hearing that voice in my head. So, I eventually began to make arrangements for my journey to Los Angeles, California. My positive thinking kicked in, and I started to see it as an adventure. "Why not?" I told myself. "I have no real victory or happiness in my life anyway. I could go and test the waters

---

[18] Paraphrased James 2:17

out there." "If things do not pan out, I can always come back home."

Although I started thinking more positively about going to Los Angeles, I preferred not to go alone. Unlike Abram, I could not find a single Lot who would agree to accompany me. All of my friends thought I had gone crazy. I did not know anyone in Los Angeles. I did not have a job lined up there. I did not even have a place to live once I got there. Never mind the recent earthquake that almost took Los Angeles off the map.

My family was offended. Many asked, "Why have you decided to go off to some strange place?" My mother was hurt. She screamed, "Who or what are you running from? Please, do not leave me!" New Orleans had been good enough for me my entire life. What was suddenly wrong with this city now?

Despite intense opposition, I packed my car with almost everything I owned and drove to Los Angeles alone. I took the 10 freeway west until it ended at Santa Monica Beach. I remember it just like it was yesterday. When I got out of my car, I felt like the Pope. I wanted to kneel down and kiss the ground. Finally, I had made it after a two and a half day drive. I looked out over the horizon and thanked God for bringing me safely to my destination.

My heart was also filled with fear and uncertainty. The only thing I knew without a doubt was for some reason I was supposed to be in Los Angeles. I stayed at a Santa Monica hotel for a few days until I found an apartment. God blessed me to land a good job in a short time. I became a stockbroker at an investment banking firm in Beverly Hills. Months later I met and married my husband, Tyrone. The rest is history.

I resigned from the last full time job I ever intend to work October 15, 1998. April 30, 2000, Tyrone did the same. We have eliminated approximately $100,000 of debt (primarily on one salary between 1996 and 1999). We could no longer afford to spend forty hours of our time every week working for someone else, because we make so much more money doing what God called us to do. God has blessed us beyond our wildest dreams. *"He is able to do exceedingly, abundantly, above what we ask or imagine, according to the power that works in us."*[19] Today we are both in full time ministry, living our lives on purpose. *"All things do work together for good to those who love God, to those who are the called according to His purpose."*[20]

This does not mean that only good things will happen. Bad things do happen to good people. During my first year in Los Angeles I had my purse stolen, I totaled my car and I was brutally attacked. Some things we cause and some things are brought by Satan, but God is always in control. Mature Christians are able to see God's presence, power and protection during the tough times. He admonishes us to *"be strong and of good courage; do not be afraid, nor be dismayed, for the Lord your God is with you wherever you go" (Joshua 1:9).* "And the Lord, He is the One who goes before you. He will be with you, He will never leave you nor forsake you; do not fear nor be dismayed."[21]

Do not be afraid to pursue your God-given purpose. Our Pastor, Bishop Charles E. Blake often says, "God protects where He directs and God provides where He guides." Go after your purpose with a vengeance. Chase it day and night. Our Lord and Savior, Jesus Christ encourages us. *"So I say to you, ask, and it will be given to you; seek, and you will find; knock, and it will be opened to you. For everyone who asks receives, and he who seeks finds, and to him who knocks it will be opened" (Luke 11:9,10).*

---

[19] Ephesians 3:20
[20] Romans 8:28
[21] Paraphrased Deuteronomy 31:8

We cannot guarantee that the road will be smooth or painless. In fact, struggles are probable. Nevertheless, you will have a richer, more meaningful and eternally blessed reality when you live your life on purpose.

We believe that God has the eye of a jeweler. Right now, you may be a diamond in the rough that He is fashioning into a priceless gem. Behold, you are work in progress.

> "When you agree to become who He sees you to be, He removes anything that isn't of diamond quality and fashions you into His shape and character so you can reflect His light.
>
> The trouble is, it can hurt to be faceted and polished. So say "Ouch" if you like, and maybe God will not put so much pressure on you. But then, He knows what you can take. Perhaps His steady but firm hand reveals more faith in you than you have in yourself.
>
> You show what you are made of as unexpected circumstances reshape your plans. Your mettle and faith get tested as you reassure yourself of a commitment and belief in a finished design."[22]

"Being confident of this very thing, that He who has begun a good work in you will complete it until the day of Jesus Christ" (Philippians 1:6). Become a person of purpose.

---

[22] Sayler, Mary H.
1995 First Days of Marriage: Day 40: Broadman and Holman Publishers: Nashville, Tennessee: page 82

Chapter 6

Inheriting Money:

A Matter Of Give And Take

A good man leaves an inheritance to his children's children.... Proverbs 13:22

Inheritance is a method of obtaining money. Since the beginning of time individuals have obtained money, property and other possessions through inheritance. According to *Webster's*, inherit means to come into possession of especially as a right or title descendible by law from an ancestor at his death; also to receive as a transmissible devise or legacy. Inheritance is the acquisition of a possession, condition, trait, tradition or heritage from past generations.[1]

There are two sides to the inheritance coin; a giver and a receiver. Let's first examine the receiver. He faces a win-lose situation regarding inheritance.

The Winner Is Also The Loser

The receiver gains a legacy, but he loses the loved one who is responsible for his gain. He derives a benefit and suffers a loss, both in the same transaction. Love and companionship cannot be replaced with tangibles, regardless of their monetary value. The receiver is left bereaved.

Grief is a heart-felt emotion. It is a normal, human response to the loss of a significant relationship. The death of a parent, friend or even a pet can be the source of grief.

---

[1] *Webster's New Collegiate Dictionary*
1981 G. & C. Merriam Company: Springfield, Massachusetts

Tragically, many do not properly grieve the loss of parents and loved ones because they feud with others by asserting their right to inherit the estate of the deceased. These family feuds tend to permanently damage and sometimes destroy existing relationships between surviving bereaved individuals. Things can get very ugly, even when the deceased made explicit provisions which are legally binding, such as a last will and testament.*

An heir is one who receives an inheritance of a deceased person by operation of law or by virtue of a will.[2] Although the realm of an inheritance can be broad, the heir has virtually no control over what, when or how much she receives. Additionally, she may be restricted in her use of the inheritance. For example: Uncle Willard left his niece, Debra $30,000 to pay for her wedding. Perhaps uncle Willard was like a father to Debra and wanted to be a part of her big day even if he was not alive to see it.

In any case, Debra's use of this money is restricted to the purpose of financing her wedding. Until Debra is engaged and begins to make plans and arrangements for the ceremony, that $30,000 inheritance remains in a trust account for safekeeping. She cannot withdraw money from this account to repair her car or to pay her college tuition, no matter how badly she needs it. Debra's inheritance from uncle Willard is designated for her wedding expenses only.

Similarly, Debra might have expressed a desire for uncle Willard's valuable coin collection. If Uncle Willard left no provision for the collection, his next closest heir would inherit it. So, cousin Bart would receive the collection instead of Debra. Neither Bart nor Debra can override uncle Willard's

---

* Legal battles abound contesting wills by claiming that the deceased individuals were incompetent at the time of designation.

[2] *Webster's New Collegiate Dictionary*
1981 G. & C. Merriam Company: Springfield, Massachusetts

designation or the legal process. Thus, the receiver has little or no control over the boundaries of his or her inheritance.

Satisfaction Not Guaranteed

Again, the receiver has little or no control over the boundaries of his or her inheritance. We find it necessary to repeat that statement because many people choose to live irresponsibly and squander their money based on their belief that they will receive an inheritance of wealth from an older relative. Unfortunately, no inheritance is guaranteed. Remember the saying, 'Tomorrow is promised to no one.' It is true. Proverbs 27:1 warns us, "*Do not boast about tomorrow, for you do not know what a day may bring forth.*" The possibilities are endless. You might predecease your elder. Your elder could leave everything to another person. Your elder may not possess anything of real monetary value at the time of death. Finally, you may be surprised to receive an inheritance from one of your contemporaries.

In Genesis 25:5,6, Abraham left all that he had to Isaac. But while he was still living, Abraham gave gifts to his other sons.[3] If Isaac had depended upon inheriting his father, Abraham's entire estate, he would have been disappointed. After all Isaac was the son God promised Abraham, not the others. Bear in mind, no inheritance is guaranteed. It does not matter what you deserve or what you are promised. The bottom line is, you do not always get what you want. Hopefully, you want what you get.

Sometimes the receiver has no concept of or appreciation for his inheritance. For instance: Isaac had two sons named Esau and Jacob. They were fraternal twins. We can imply from the scriptures that Isaac's wife, Rebekah had a

---

[3] Paraphrased Genesis 25:5,6

difficult pregnancy, *"the two children struggled within her" (Genesis 25:22).* Esau was the first-born which meant that he would become the head of the family when Isaac died. It also meant that Esau would receive a double share of his father's inheritance. This was a Jewish custom and a great honor.[4]

Apparently Esau thought very little of his birthright. Once when Jacob was cooking some stew, Esau came in from the open country, famished. He said to Jacob, "Quick, let me have some of that red stew! I'm famished!"

> "First sell me your birthright," Jacob replied.
>
> "Look, I am about to die," Esau said. "What good is the birthright to me?"
>
> But Jacob said, "Swear to me first."

So he swore an oath to him, selling his birthright to Jacob. Then Jacob gave Esau some bread and some lentil stew. He ate and drank, and then got up and left. So Esau despised his birthright.[5]

During this time a verbal oath was all that was required to make the transaction legal. Esau lusted for the present and tangible at any cost. His brother Jacob, though obviously deceitful in his tactics, truly respected the right to his father's inheritance.

It is hard to resist the temptation to criticize Esau's foolish decision. Yet, many of us make the same choice on a daily basis. Esau had the 'buy now pay later' mentality that is prevalent today. We want what we want and we want it now! We expect immediate gratification. Most people do not want to wait for that pot of gold at the end of the rainbow. If they

[4] Deuteronomy 21:17
[5] Genesis 25:29-34 New International Version

did, credit card companies would be extinct. Instead we pull money out of our retirement accounts early to buy our 'stew' of choice incurring penalties that considerably decrease the value of our nest egg. We compromise our health and our wealth for a quick fix.

There was another young man in the Bible who had a modern-day approach to his inheritance. He chose not to wait until after his father died. He decided to take matters into his own hands. The story is found in Luke 15:11-32. It is entitled, The Prodigal Son. Here we share the beginning of this story. "*A certain man had two sons. And the younger of them said to his father, 'Father, give me the portion of goods that falls to me.' So he divided to them his livelihood. And not many days after, the younger son gathered all together, journeyed to a far country, and there wasted his possessions with prodigal living. But when he had spent all, there arose a severe famine in that land, and he began to be in want" (Luke 15:11-14).*

The prodigal son thought he had things all figured out, just as many of us do. This story teaches us a valuable lesson. If a person has not learned how to manage effectively what God has entrusted to him, obtaining more will not help him. Such a person may acquire more, but he will probably continue to squander it until he eventually loses everything. More than likely, this person has a 'happy-go-lucky' or 'easy come easy go' attitude toward money. He fails to count the cost.

Often our relatives and friends ask us for loans. We have adopted the policy not to loan money to our loved ones. Some interpret this as a tough position. It does not mean that we do not love these individuals. They are very important to us. In fact, we take this position because we love them.

We would do everything within our power to insure that the special people in our lives are equipped with the necessities: adequate food, clothing and shelter. Many times we give them money. That is correct, we said give, not loan. We only part with an amount of money we can afford to give away, even if that amount is significantly less than what he or she has asked of us.

When someone approaches you in need of money, you have to question what brought that individual to such a point. Perhaps he made bad business decisions or maybe he simply developed poor spending habits. Could he be living above and beyond his means? In chapter two we described what happens to excessive-living-feast-mentality individuals.

Regardless of what caused his condition, why would he treat the money you give him any different than he does his own money? If he spends too much money, he will spend yours too. If he practices an indebted lifestyle, what's one more person to owe? If he is not a good businessman, your money will not suddenly make him a Wall Street tycoon. And if he is busy 'keeping up with the Joneses,' he will continue in that vein until he has nothing. Think about it. He may want your money to pay a debt he cannot afford to pay. If that is the case, how will he pay you back? He could be depending on someone else to pay him so that he will be able to pay you back. Should you rely on the credibility of someone you do not know? Getting caught in this vicious cycle makes you an accomplice. Money can be like a loaded gun. If you give it to someone who does not know how to use it, he is bound to hurt himself and his injury could be fatal. Bankers know this instinctively.*

We are not in the habit of flushing our hard-earned money down the toilet, in the name of love. We prefer to educate others and help them change their lives. Sometimes

---

* Lenders closely examine whether an applicant is a good or bad credit risk. Most loans require collateral; the applicant must place something of his own at stake. For more details refer to book two of our trilogy, Escape from Debtors Prison: *LET MY PEOPLE GO!*

tough love is the best method of accomplishing that. We pray that our loved ones never need to come to us or anyone else for money. Proverbs 22:7 says "*The borrower is servant to the lender.*" We do not want our loved ones to be slaves to anyone, ourselves included.

Deborah Smith Pegues gives advise on handling the '*leeches*' we all know and love.

> A relative or friend has borrowed money from you and has conveniently forgotten to repay you again. You resent the fact the she lives above her means while you often forego certain pleasures to save money. She now finds herself in another financial jam and needs to "borrow a little change." You have decided to put a stop to it.

* Be a broken record in saying "no."

* Realize that by always bailing the person out, you are enabling the person to remain irresponsible.

* Don't leave the door open for a future request by saying you don't have the money this time.

* Refuse to be manipulated or made to feel guilty.[6]

Few of us remember our infant years. However, most of us have spent time with small children. If you carry a baby around all the time, he gets very comfortable in your arms. He has no motivation to try to walk on his own. At some point, you have to step back and allow him to stand on his own two

---

[6] Pegues, Deborah Smith
1997 *Managing Conflict God's Way*: New Kensington, PA: Whitaker House: page 183.

feet. Sure, he may fall a few times. But once he's ready, he will walk. That baby will be so excited to find his new independence. Soon he will run and eventually you will have trouble keeping up with him. That is the vision of POTTS, Intl. We usher people into financial independence.

Good Or Bad Inheritance

Now let's observe the role of the giver. Proverbs 13:22 says "*A good man leaves an inheritance to his children's children.*" This scripture is referring to a good person leaving a valuable inheritance to not only his children but to his grandchildren as well. Remember an inheritance can be a possession, condition, trait, tradition or heritage from past generations.[7]

An inheritance may not always be good. An individual could inherit undesirables from his elder. Medical research substantiates the fact that many diseases and ill health conditions are hereditary. Also, parents pass bad habits down to their children. Time after time we find the, 'Do as I say not as I do' instruction of parents to be virtually ineffective child rearing. Children tend to follow their parents' lead and model the behavior they witness.

The deceased person could leave his family and inheritance of unpaid bills. In this case, the heirs would be forced to pay the debt out of his remaining estate. You can imagine the burden of such an inheritance. People are not thrilled to pay their own debts. The pain of paying someone else's tab just to obtain the leftovers (if there are any) can be excruciating.

In the Bible we find even more extreme retribution demanded from the family of a man who died in debt. *A widow*

---

[7] *Webster's New Collegiate Dictionary*
1981 G. & C. Merriam Company: Springfield, Massachusetts

cried out to the prophet, "Your servant my husband is dead...now his creditor is coming to take my two boys as his slaves." The prophet asked what she had in her house. "Your servant has nothing there at all," she said, "except a little oil" (2 Kings 4:1,2).[8]

The prophet was able to bless the widow and help her out of this horrible situation. Many times we find ourselves in the same predicament. A relative can die without enough money in his estate to pay for his own funeral or burial. The grief stricken and bereaved heirs have to scrape up the money to lay their loved one to rest. This is the worst time for money to be an issue.

What Will You Leave Behind?

Last chapter we discussed purpose, what we were created to do on this earth. Your purpose includes what the world is left with when you have gone to be with God. Several questions arise when someone is faced with his or her own mortality. How will I be remembered? Will my loved ones gain any knowledge from my life? Did I reach my full potential and accomplish all that God designed me to do? Will anyone follow in my footsteps? Can someone find the meaning in my life?

Dr. Jerry Horner relays his rendition of a celebrated biography that summarizes the life span of a myriad of people. "Years ago I read a biography:

Solomon Grunday ...
Born on Monday ...
Christened on Tuesday ...
Married on Wednesday ...

[8] Paraphrased 2 Kings 1,2

Taken ill on Thursday ...
Worse on Friday ...
Died on Saturday ...
Buried on Sunday ...
And that was the end of Solomon Grunday."[9]

The wealthiest spot on this planet is not the oil fields of Kuwait, Iraq or Saudi Arabia. Neither is it the gold, diamond or silver mines of Africa, or the uranium mines of the Soviet Union. Though it may surprise you, the richest deposits on our planet lie just few blocks from your house. They rest in your local cemetery or graveyard. Buried beneath the soil within the walls of those sacred grounds are dreams that never came to pass, songs that were never sung, books that were never written, paintings that never became reality, inventions that were never designed, plans that never went beyond the drawing board of the mind and purposes that were never fulfilled. Our graveyards are filled with potential that remained potential. What a tragedy![10]

Only you can decide if you are going to rob the world or bless it. A good man leaves a good inheritance, not only to his children, but also to his grandchildren and the generations to come.[11] What will you leave behind? Take some time to sit down and contemplate the things that are really most important to you. Your list may surprise you. Mine sure did.

I once taught a teen Sunday school class. One day I gave my students an assignment to write their own obituaries. In order to complete this assignment, they had to carefully consider all the things they wanted to accomplish in a lifetime.

---

[9] Munroe, Myles
1991 *Understanding Your Potential*: Foreword by Dr. Jerry Horner: Destiny Image Publishers: Shippenburg, PA
[10] Ibid.
[11] Paraphrased Proverbs 13:22

They also needed to take into account other people's feelings toward them. This assignment was so profound that I decided to complete one for myself. I recommend that you do the same. You have creative license to construct it anyway you desire. I am sure it will make a significant impact upon your life. It certainly did for me.

I wrote my obituary in the form of a poem, because I love poetry. I will share it now. I pray that you find it encouraging and inspiring.

Bury Me In My Best Red Dress

When I die, bury me in my best red dress
For I have lived a full and vibrant life
Spare me the solemn, dignified wake
Where the choir sings sad hymns
And my loved ones shed sorrowful tears
Instead go outside and sound the trumpets
Parade through the streets
Dance until your feet can no longer carry you
Mourn as I have lived
Please do this for me

When I die, bury me in my best red dress
Don't sit around crying because I am gone
For I gave this world everything I had to offer
I leave proudly, in peace and joy
Embracing the eternal life which has long awaited
My arrival on the other side of glory
Mourn as I have lived
Please do this for me

When I die bury me in my best red dress
Be blessed to live and to leave as I have

For I embraced life to the fullest
Defying logic every chance I got
I traveled alone to far away lands
Where I did not know a soul
I climbed mountains
When I despised heights
I went skiing and snow-boarding
My very first time in the snow
I went parasailing and jet-skiing
Before learning how to swim
I ran marathons just because
I laughed when it was inappropriate
And I cried when it was unexpected
I rose to every challenge and adventure
That bore my name
Mourn as I have lived
Please do this for me

When I die bury me in my best red dress
For my life has been full and most rewarding
I utilized every gift the Lord gave me
I fed the hungry with food I prepared with my own hands
I clothed the naked with clothes from my own closet
I prayed for people I did not know
I taught the teachable
I counseled those in turmoil
I cared for the sick
And I calmed the angry
When I was wronged by others, I forgave them
When I wronged others, I repented and asked forgiveness
I tried to express gratitude and grace in dismal situations
Mourn as I have lived
Please do this for me

When I die bury me in my best red dress
For I embraced everything that was me
I relished in my strengths
And I tried to minimize my shortcomings
Sometimes I suffered in silence
Other times I kicked and screamed every step of the way
I took long walks on the beach with God
I stayed up all night talking to my family
I journeyed for miles and miles just to help a friend
I loved and married a wonderful man
I bore and raised terrific children
My house was filled with laughter and singing
I thank God for every day he blessed me with
Every person I met
Every problem I conquered
Every life that was changed just cause our paths crossed
Mourn as I have lived
Please do this for me

So when I die, bury me in my best red dress
For I have lived a full and vibrant life
Spare me the solemn, dignified wake
Where the choir sings sad hymns
And my loved ones shed sorrowful tears
Instead go outside and sound the trumpets
Parade through the streets
Dance until your feet can no longer carry you
Mourn as I have lived
Please do this for me

- Rachelle A. Potts

Like an onion, you must peel away those superficial layers in order to get down to the bare essentials. I realized that it did not matter where I went to school, what academic degrees I obtained, the jobs or titles I held, the cars I drove, the houses I lived in or the amount of money in my bank account. What mattered most to me was hearing Him say, *"Well done my good and faithful servant...Enter into the joy of your Lord" (Matthew 25:21).*[12]

What is most important to you? Leave behind a good inheritance that will make your creator proudly welcome you into His loving arms.

---

[12] Paraphrased Matthew 25:21

Chapter 7

Who Wants To Be A Millionaire?

And everyone who competes for the prize is temperate in all things. Now they do it to obtain a perishable crown; but we for an imperishable crown. 1 Corinthians 9:25

Winning money has become extremely popular in today's society. Game shows are sweeping the nation and everyone is caught up in millionaire mania. "Who doesn't want to be a millionaire? The latest craze in million-dollar game shows has the country dreaming and hoping about striking it rich."[1]

Winning money can be a wonderful and exhilarating method of obtaining additional income. However, some cash prizes present pitfalls. As Christians, we should carefully consider how we obtain money. Our integrity and virtue should be without question, because we represent Christ. Every manner in which we obtain money sends a message to the world, and there are certain types of messages we definitely do not want to send.

There are three basic categories of winnings:
free fun, charity, gambling.

---

[1] Oprah Winfrey
2000 When You're the Millionaire in the Family: National Talk Show Broadcast: Harpo Productions: Aired February 25, 2000

The Best Things In Life Are Free

Contests and game shows fall in the category called free fun. Do you remember the pie-eating contest at the county fair? Uncle Buck entered every year. He did not mind drinking a gallon of the 'pink stuff' afterward, as long as he maintained his title of reigning champion. Uncle Buck prided himself on being the most skilled pie eater this side of Broward county.

Contestant opportunities are endless. Who has not dreamed of Ed McMahan knocking at his door with a great big check from Publishers Clearing House. Many people fill out a stack of entry forms as thick as the yellow pages and subscribe to magazines they do not read for a chance to win a million dollars.

Television game shows take this friendly competition concept to a new dimension. Millions of eyes stay glued to their television sets for hours in hope of seeing an average person become an instant millionaire. Tensions heighten and anxiety mounts as questions of increasing difficulty are answered by an 'extraordinary' contestant. Viewers have one question on their minds, *Will he do it?*

Though it does not happen every day, it has happened to several individuals. David won $1.7 million on the game show "Twenty One." Curtis won $1.4 million on the game show "Greed." John, Dan, Joe and Bob all won $1 million dollars on the game show "Who Wants To Be A Millionaire?" Members of the viewing audience remain faithful because they believe, *If it can happen for them, surely it can happen for me.*

In Houston, civil engineer Robert Gordon, 40, says, "It's obvious why 'Who Wants To Be A Millionaire?' is popular. This is the type of show that will succeed because everyone that watches will love to see someone like themselves at least has the chance to get rich."[2] Steven Stark, author of "Glued to the Set: The 60 Television Shows and Events That Made Us Who We Are Today," says "People get to see people like themselves on TV, and that's always been an incredible draw,"[3] Bob Boden, co-creator of Fox's "Greed" says, "There's a certain thrill to being part of a shared national experience and that's part of the reason why these shows have caught on." "Everyone at home wants to be one of those people winning, so the level of identification and empathy with contestants is phenomenal."[4]

We've heard stories about how people try day after day and all hours of the night to qualify to become contestants on these highly rated game shows. If we put that much effort and energy into everything, the world would be a better place. Please do not mistake my comment. There is nothing wrong with playing a game that tests your intelligence, aptitude or speed. Investing time in educating yourself about any note-worthy subject can finally pay off. Alex Trebek, host of Jeopardy, says "It's fashionable to be bright nowadays. On our show, it's skills, it's quick reflexes, it's broad knowledge, and now with shows like Millionaire and Greed, you have the added allure of big money."[5]

The big pay-off, however, belongs to the network. The networks have discovered what the Las Vegas and Atlantic City mobs have known for decades; a great way to make tons of money is to give it away. ABC will win far more millions than "Who Want's To Be A Millionaire?" contestants. The show is by far the network's biggest money-maker in

---

[2] Puente, Maria
1999 USA Today: Hooked On 'Millionaire' Cover Story:11/17/99
[3] Ibid.
[4] Puente, Maria
1999 USA Today: Hooked On 'Millionaire' Cover Story:11/17/99
[5] Ibid.

years. It costs roughly $400,000 an hour to air the show, just one-third the rate for an average prime time drama. Yet advertisers are paying an average of $300,000 for each 30-second commercial. That translates into $6 million in advertising revenue per hour.[6]

Why are advertisers willing to pay top dollar? Because we all are watching and ratings ultimately determine the advertising dollar value. The viewer audience tally has been outstanding. November 8-14, 1999 (only one week of broadcasting), "Who Wants To Be A Millionaire?" had more than 112 million viewers.[7] Advertisers reach out to the masses, and they know exactly where to find them.

Apparently, much of the USA is addicted to "Who Wants To Be A Millionaire?" the high-tech, multiple-choice quiz show, hosted by Regis Philbin, where contestants answer a series of 15 questions leading, potentially, to a million dollar win.[8]

Even ivory-tower denizens watch television, including TV game shows such as "Who Wants To Be A Millionaire?" the ABC phenomenon now sweeping the ratings, the country and otherwise rational people off their feet.[9]

Robert Thompson, director of Syracuse's Center for the Study of Popular Television, said "It's almost impossible to quit watching, it's so compelling. It is the programming equivalent of crack cocaine."[10] Wow, what an analogy!

---

[6] Levin, Gary

1999 USA Today: "Making Million$ ABC discovers that a great way to make tons of money is to give it away" Cover Story: 11/5/99

[7] Puente, Maria

1999 USA Today: Hooked on 'Millionaire' Cover Story: 11/17/99

[8] Ibid.

[9] Puente, Maria

1999 USA Today: Hooked on 'Millionaire' Cover Story: 11/17/99

[10] Ibid.

Contests and game shows afford the participants fun and an opportunity to win valuable prizes. Best of all, there is no cost to enter. Sure you run the risk of losing miserably. You might even walk away embarrassed about the experience. It takes courage to allow yourself to be vulnerable before millions of viewers. Though millions are willing to watch, make comments and form opinions about you; few have the nerve to put themselves on the line. A vast majority of people remain in the safe spectator role. Viewers may identify with the contestants, but they cannot share the prizes. If you do not try, you cannot win. Thus, your presence automatically makes you a winner among the masses. My husband, Tyrone always says, "You have to be in it to win it."

Contestants must be good sports. True sportsmanship is the ability to laugh at yourself, never forgetting that it is just a game. No one likes a sore loser or a sore winner either. A sore loser drowns in his own self-pity. He finds solace in blaming others for his poor showing. On the other hand, a sore winner is cocky and condescending. He displays little or no humility. He rants and raves about his feat. A sore winner also puts others down in order to make himself look better. He never acknowledges that he had a worthy opponent. He must be sole king, ruler and master of the universe. He is the greatest, while everyone else is merely mortal. This is the guy we love to hate. In fact, we support anyone willing to challenge him.

God can use contests and game shows to bless his people. Sometimes Christians place limits on God. It is as if we expect Him to rain money down on us like manna from heaven. God can make that happen. However, He uses all kinds of people and all sorts of opportunities to bless His children. We simply have to be more willing to avail ourselves of this magnitude of resources.

Many times fear and self-doubt hold us back. We are afraid that we will look silly or foolish. We are afraid of what others might think or say about us. We are afraid of potential humiliation, failure and in some cases even success. We must learn to say "so what!" So what, if I look silly. So what, if I am embarrassed or someone calls me foolish. That person will just have to get over it. Who cares what he thinks anyway. I care about what God thinks. We are the Body of Christ, and God thinks the world of us. He loved us so much that, He placed all things under our feet.[11] "*For God has not given us a spirit of fear, but of power and of love and of a sound mind" (2 Timothy 1:7).* Learn to laugh in the face of your fears. God has a good sense of humor and so should we.

I will admit that I was not born this way. There was a time when I became embarrassed very easily. I wore my heart on my sleeve, and I was extremely sensitive to the thoughts and views of others. God used the Beta Gamma Chapter of Delta Sigma Theta sorority to strengthen this weakness. I benefited greatly from the pledge experience. I did ridiculous things to reach my goal. At times I became so frustrated, I would burst into tears for no apparent reason. I learned the meaning of endurance, determination and perseverance. I decided not to let others stop me from pursuing my purpose. In many ways, I became my own woman. I still have fears. I just move forward in spite of my fears. If you think that fear is an obstacle in your life, ask God to strengthen you in this area. He still answers prayers. *"Therefore I say to you, whatever things you ask when you pray, believe that you receive them, and you will have them" (Mark 11:24).*

In 1997, Tyrone and I were contestants on the Newlywed Game. Although we lost, we had fun. We did not complain or pout. As a matter of fact, we sent the production crew a thank you card and a box of chocolates. God told

[11] Paraphrased Ephesians 1:22

Tyrone that we were going back on that show. Sure enough, several months later, the show contacted us and asked us to participate in an alumni taping. We were delighted to go on the show again. That time we won. So in 1998, we enjoyed an all-expense-paid, weeklong second honeymoon in Maui, Hawaii.

Additionally, in 1999 we went on the Family Feud game show and won $10,000. Our winnings are the result of God's divine favor and blessing. As soon as our schedules permit, we plan to audition for another game show.

Action and involvement come easy to some. Others have to make a conscious effort. Dr. Jerry Horner says "People generally fall into one of three groups: the few who make things happen, the many who watch things happen and the overwhelming majority who have no notion of what happens."[12] Ouch!

Clearly, God can bless you too with trips, cash, even cars and other valuable prizes through contests and game shows. However, the odds of winning a big game show are astronomically slim. Even getting on one is a long shot. You must be up for the challenge. Although the best things in life are free, they usually do not come easily. Sometimes you may win and other times you may lose. Yet, you will never know unless you try. Regardless of the outcome, it is always a blessing to get up off the bench or the sidelines of life and become a real player.

"The only way to discover the limits of the possible is to go beyond them into the impossible." - Arthur C. Clarke

---

[12] Munroe, Myles
1991 *Understanding Your Potential*: Foreword by Dr. Jerry Horner: Destiny Image Publishers: Shippenburg, PA

"I can do all things through Christ who strengthens me" (Philippians 4:13).

The Good Cause Trap

Charity is another category of winning. Raffles and Friday night bingo are in this group. Good causes are all over the place. You never have to look very long to find one. They find you.

Many times people ask others to purchase a raffle ticket to support a school fund-raiser or a community based non-profit organization. The response is usually yes, because it is such a small amount and it will benefit a good cause. That raffle ticket indicates the date and time of the drawing and prizes that will be given away. Frequently there is a cash prize much greater than the ticket price. In essence, you have purchased a chance to win $500, $1,000 or more depending upon the size of the fund-raiser.

This charitable contribution process is a dangerous gray area for Christians. Of course we want to support good causes. However, purchasing something that does not deliver you a good or service crosses the thin line between charity and gambling. Gambling by definition means to stake something on a contingency; to play a game of chance for money or other stakes; to bet on an uncertain outcome.[13] When you bought that ticket for a chance to win the prize, you gambled.

You may ask, 'Is anything wrong with gambling?' We will address the subject of gambling in more detail next section. For now a better question would be "Should Christians gamble?" In Deuteronomy 6 :16, Moses directed the Israelites, *"You shall not tempt the Lord your God."*

---

[13] *Webster's New Collegiate Dictionary*
1981 G. & C. Merriam Company: Springfield, Massachusetts

Again in Luke 4:12, Jesus reiterated, *"It has been said, 'You shall not tempt the Lord your God.'"*

In the Bible, the sacred lot was cast as a means of determining the mind of God.[14] In ancient Israel it was assumed that God was in control of the dice and that He would speak to His people this way. Although there is no such thing as luck and God is in control of everything, when somebody takes money that belongs to God (because everything we have belongs to God) and bets it on the turn of a roulette wheel, or a turn of a card, he is asking for trouble.[15] He is saying by his actions, "God, I am risking Your money and my faith on the hope that You'll 'make it happen!'" When you act like that, you are putting the Lord to the test. You are tempting God, and that is sin.[16] Gambling is tempting God. Christians should not tempt God. Therefore, Christians should not gamble.

Gambling can destroy a person, becoming an obsession and a compulsion just like alcoholism. The habitual gambler ruins his family and his life, and some have stolen to get money for gambling. It can become a disease that has destroyed literally tens of thousands of people.[17]

The pervasiveness of gambling in our society teaches people that fame, success, and fortune are available without work or struggle. The virtues of industry, thrift, careful investment, and patience are all undermined by this vice. In their place come human greed, lust, avarice, sloth, and a live-for-the-moment mentality. How tragic to see legislatures link

---

[14] Leviticus 16:7-10; Jonah 1:7 and Acts 1:24-26

[15] Robertson, Pat
1984 *Answers to 200 of Life's Most Probing Questions*: Thomas Nelson Publishing, Inc: Nashville, TN

[16] Deuteronomy 6:16 and Luke 4:12

[17] Robertson, Pat
1984 Answers to 200 of Life's Most Probing Questions: Thomas Nelson Publishing, Inc: Nashville, TN

their budgetary futures to legalized gambling and lotteries that will undermine the very virtues their citizens need for true long-range growth and prosperity![18]

If you want to support the elementary school or the community center, write them a check. We prefer to give a donation instead of purchasing a ticket. They gladly accept it and appreciate it.

It is also a good idea to become a member of the Parent Teacher Association, vote on issues before the community advisory board or volunteer at the senior center. Most good causes need your active participation more than your money, so get involved. You will find that people in these good cause groups plan raffles to raise funds because they have not been taught the negative implications of gambling. Will you be the one to explain? If you do not, some may never learn the truth.

The lottery started off as a good cause. Many states instituted lotteries to support schools. Educating children is certainly a very good cause. Yet, every election period we face several propositions designed to direct more and more of our tax dollars toward education. My question is, "Where on earth is all that lottery money going?"

Now let us examine the Friday night bingo scenario. Some churches and religious organizations have a bingo or game night. All proceeds go to the church. I personally do not believe that you will go to hell for occasionally playing bingo on Friday night at the neighborhood church or community center. But then again, I do not have a heaven or a hell to put you in. This is something you really need to pray about.

---

[18] Robertson, Pat
1984 *Answers to 2000 of Life's Most Probing Questions*: Thomas Nelson Publishing, Inc: Nashville, TN

If you go there to meet friends because you find it a socially entertaining and safe environment to have good clean fun, God is probably fine with that. He knows your heart. "*For the Lord does not see as man sees, for man looks at the outward appearance, but the Lord looks at the heart" (1 Samuel 16:7).* Are you sure that you do this for the right reasons? Ask God. "*Search me, O God, and know my heart. Try me, and know my thoughts. And see if there is any wicked way in me. And lead me in the way everlasting" (Psalms 139:23,24).*[19]

Technically you are deriving the benefit of a social gathering place and entertainment just as you would at the skating rink. Perhaps you receive a door prize or free refreshments when you purchase a bingo card. You must be careful, however, that you are not involved in the process solely to win. Bad things can result from activities that are intended to be fun. Bingo closely resembles gambling. As we mentioned earlier, this behavior is dangerously addictive and perpetuates compulsion. Proceed with caution.

Additionally, Christians should consider others. We are the representatives of Christ. Maybe Sharon is not prone to succumb to the vice of gambling, but her friend Jane is weak in this area. For Sharon to suggest that they attend Friday night bingo would be unwise. The temptation would be too strong for Jane to refuse. Besides, Jane views Sharon as a good Christian role model. She may conclude, 'If Sharon supports this, it must be alright.' In Romans 14:21, Apostle Paul says it is better not to eat meat, drink wine or do anything else that will cause your brother to stumble or by which your brother is offended or made weak.[20] Your life may be the only Bible some people ever read. "*Abstain from all appearance of evil"*

---

[19] Paraphrased Psalm 139:23,24

[20] Paraphrased Romans 14:21

(1 Thessalonians 5:22).[21] Remember others are watching, do not give them the wrong impression of Christ.

Odds Not In Your Favor

We discussed the free fun category of winning that is acceptable behavior for Christians. Contests and game shows qualify as free fun, because you do not have to pay money to participate. We also examined the activities that closely resemble gambling. Raffles and bingo are borderline gray areas that easily and frequently tread into suspect territory.

Some activities, however, that cannot be mistaken for anything but gambling. Lotteries, casino style gaming, other forms of betting like office pools, and wagers on horse races are all blatant gambling. We have discovered that gambling is sinful, undesired behavior because it tempts God. Therefore, Christians should never participate in these activities.

Unfortunately, many Christians gamble. My question is, "Why?" Gambling brings more harm than any good that might be derived from it.

I grew up in New Orleans, Louisiana. During the early 1990's, state officials reinstituted legalized gambling in New Orleans, promising that casinos would bring in new revenues and enhance the economy of the city. I was a member of the small minority who fought against this plan, but we lost to the majority.

As a resident of New Orleans, I did not notice many major economic improvements brought by the gaming industry. However, I did witness a considerable increase in criminal activity. In the last section, I called gambling a sin, because it tempts God. The Bible teaches that sin begets more sin.[22] After the gaming industry came to New Orleans, I saw

---

[21] 1 Thessalonians 5:22 King James Version

[22] Romans 5:12

more incidents of robbery, car theft, burglary, murder, drug abuse, rape and sexual assault. Consequently, the character of the city experienced a significant decline. I agree with the politicians, "Gambling can transform a city." Gambling makes it worse.

New Orleans and other small cities that provide legalized gambling are small fries compared to the glamour and glitz of Las Vegas and Atlantic City. People all around the world travel to these well-known cities that never sleep. The almighty slot machine, the roulette wheel and the black jack table draw in masses of tourists. Food and other essentials are considerably cheaper in Las Vegas and Atlantic City, because the gaming industry understands that tourists will spend most of their money and time gambling in the casinos.

Las Vegas, Nevada is widely recognized as the gambling capital of the world. As a result, prostitution is legal in the state of Nevada. There is no question about the impact of gambling.

What It Costs To Gamble

The California SuperLOTTO consists of picking six numbers. The numbers chosen must range from 1 through 51 without duplication. Given these parameters, the mathematical probability of picking the six winning numbers can be precisely calculated.

The following equation states the exact odds of winning:

$$(51/6)x(50/5)x(49/4)x(48/3)x(47/2)x(46/1)= 18,009,460$$

Which means:

51 choices divided by 6 picks multiplied by
50 choices divided by 5 picks multiplied by
49 choices divided by 4 picks multiplied by
48 choices divided by 3 picks multiplied by
47 choices divided by 2 picks multiplied by
46 choices divided by 1 pick

Or

$$8.5 \times 10 \times 12.25 \times 16 \times 23.5 \times 46 = 18{,}009{,}460$$

The California SuperLOTTO game instruction sheet indicates that the odds of picking all six numbers correctly are 1 in 18,009,460.

Now let us put these odds in the proper perspective. According to the U.S. Census Bureau, the adult population of the state of California as of July 1, 1999, was 24,221,698 (individuals at least 18 years old). Therefore, if every adult bought one ticket, only 1[*] of the total 24,221,698 people would probably pick the right numbers! Needless to say, the chances of winning the grand prize are extremely remote. For this reason weeks pass without anyone winning, and the jackpot rises to an astronomical multi-million dollar figure.

Unfortunately, there is a positive correlation between the size of the jackpot and the number of tickets sold. The higher the jackpot the more tickets sold. We attribute this to greed and irrational exuberance. However, there is an inverse relationship between the number of tickets sold and the chance of being the sole winner of the grand prize. The more tickets

---

[*] The solution was rounded down to the nearest whole number.

sold the less chance one has to win the whole jackpot. More participants translate into more competition.

Sadly people waste millions of dollars on the incredibly small possibility that the so called "lady luck" will smile upon them. Not only does the lottery constitute gambling, it is very addictive. Delusions of grandeur lure people into a weekly web of compulsion. The dream of what life would be like as a millionaire is used to manipulate millions into a poor investment and retirement plan.

What if you win the lottery? Would you be fortunate at all? Proverbs 1:32 states, "The prosperity of fools shall destroy them." Money does not change who you are, it only magnifies it.[*] People with bad financial habits do not suddenly change because they acquire money. Typically, they will behave exactly as they always have and, in many cases the behavior is foolish.

Winners should keep in mind that sudden wealth can also create problems. Research shows a number of big winners end up going bankrupt and gaining significant weight after winning.[23] Ultimately, they live worse than they did before their 'fortune.' We assume these people have "life styles of the rich and famous." Yet, many of Hollywood's finest and others have told the horror story of how their rise to fame did not come with an instruction manual on how to handle *Sudden Wealth Syndrome*.[*]

A corner store or market in affluent areas such as Beverly Hills seldom advertises, 'Lottery tickets here.' The reason is that lottery ticket sales thrive most in inner city

---

[*] See Chapter 2 $87 million powerball jackpot winner talks
8/30/99 Oprah Winfrey Show: Harpo Productions

[23] Sabih, Jennifer
4/9/98 CBS 2 News Special Assignment: "After The Jackpot"

[*] See Chapter 2 Jessie O'Neill addresses issues which the newly rich experience in *The Golden Ghetto: The Psychology of Affluence*

America. The biggest supporters of the lottery are those with the most to lose.

Those responsible for marketing state lotteries understand that in order to sell those tickets they must sell the dream. They also know that those most inclined to buy the dream of a life without financial concerns are the people who have the biggest financial concerns, the poor!

The California lottery slogan is, "Who's next?" This slogan implies that anyone can be next to strike it rich, and it could be you! Who's next to buy their dream home? Who's next to quit the job they hate? Who's next to buy their dream car? And who's next to take a cruise around the world? Wise people know what this slogan is really saying: Who's next to foolishly waste their money on a pipe dream? Who's next to give away money they worked so hard to earn? And who's next to throw away their precious resources that should be used to purchase necessities for their families?

Bishop Charles E. Blake, pastor of West Angeles Church of God In Christ in Los Angeles, California recently released a wonderful book entitled, *Dreamers Are Coming.* He states, "I see the strength of fantasies in the eyes of folk lining up to buy lottery tickets. Whenever the prize reaches unusually big numbers, you see regular folk-- hard- working and usually sensible folk-- succumb to lotto fever. In every community you can hear the cry of families going hungry because the grocery money went to buy lottery tickets. That's not a God-given dream! That's just greedy fantasy."[24]

Those who participate in the lottery not only condone this exploitation of the poor, they also support it. Are you one of the people who support this shameless disregard for public welfare? The California SuperLOTTO instruction form displays the clause, Play Responsibly. It also includes a

---

[24] Blake, Charles E. Sr. Bishop
1999 *Dreamers Are Coming*: Albury Publishing: Tulsa: page 17

telephone number to a gambling problem referral line: 1-888-277-3115. Unmarried people should know that the only safe sex is no sex. Similarly, Christians should know that the only responsible play is not playing at all! Practice abstinence from the lottery.

A closer look at the California SuperLOTTO instruction form reveals yet another astounding fact. The jackpot is paid in 26 annual payments! Like a familiar joke:

"Hey, I won a million dollars in the lottery."

"Hey, great!"

"Yeah, I get a dollar a year for a million years."

If you want a lump sum payment, the jackpot is reduced by 50 percent or more. To add insult to injury, consider the income taxes you will have to pay. Let us assume that you picked the six wonderful winning numbers, and the jackpot was a cool $1,000,000. If you want a lump sum payment, that $1,000,000 will be cut in half to $500,000. Uncle Sam will take his $198,000* off of the top. And if your state has an income tax requirement, there goes another bite. The lump sum $500,000 payday would translate into a maximum of $302,000! Don't start counting your chickens before they hatch. The Internal Revenue Service takes Uncle Sam's portion before you get yours. Bill collectors will have no problem reposessing whatever you cannot afford. So my advice is "let the buyer beware."

---

* This number is based on the highest federal individual income tax bracket of 39.6%

Who Really Wants To Be A Millionaire?

Do you really want to be a millionaire? Winning money and other valuables can be a fantastic experience. However, most individuals who maintain a net worth of one million dollars or more, did not acquire their wealth from a contest, game show, raffle, the race track or the state lottery. Instead they raked in their big bucks with more productive work, less wasteful spending, smarter sound investments and 'good old fashioned' discipline.

Years ago a third grader named Troy Johnson told me that he would become a millionaire as soon as he turned 18 years old. He aroused my curiosity of course. Troy attended a public school and had two working-class parents. Naturally, I began to wonder, *Where will this little boy get so much money.* I concluded that Troy must be an heir of a rich deceased relative who left him a fortune and the money was in a trust account until Troy came of age. I wanted to confirm my theory, so I asked him, "How will you become a millionaire when you turn 18 years old?"

> Troy responded, "When I turn 18, I will change my name to Michael."
>
> By now, I was very confused. "Michael?" I asked, "What does that have to do with becoming a millionaire?"

Then Troy explained, "The first people that pop into my mind when I think of millionaires are Michael Jordan and Michael Jackson. I figured, they both have the MJ names and they are both millionaires. I already have the J (Johnson) part, I just need the Michael." He continued, "I begged my parents, but they would not change my name to Michael. When I turn

18, I will be old enough to change it myself. Then, I will become a millionaire too."

It took me a long time to convince Troy Johnson that changing his first name to Michael would not make him rich. In fact, I am still not sure that he believes me.

Many of us share Troy's misconception. We think the entertainers and athletes we watch on television represent the average millionaire. Our assumption could not be more false. Yes, Michael Jordan and Michael Jackson, both African American males are millionaires, but they are the exception not the norm. In a recent national survey of millionaires, Dr. Thomas Stanley and Dr. William Danko asked the respondents to designate their country of origin/ancestry/ethnic origin. The results may surprise you.[25] The number of African American households that have a net worth of one million dollars or more are so few, that they are not even represented in the statistics for the top ten ancestry groups of American millionaires! Also, notice that Hispanics are not represented either.

---

[25] Stanley, Thomas and Danko, William Ph.Ds
1996 *The Millionaire Next Door: The Surprising Secrets of America's Wealthy*: Pocket Books: New York, NY: page 17

Table 2: The Top Ten Ancestry Groups of American Millionaires

Ancestry Group/ Ethnic Origin	**Rank**	**Ethnic Origin**	**Rank**
ENGLISH	**1**	**ITALIAN**	**6**
GERMAN	**2**	**FRENCH**	**7**
IRISH	**3**	**DUTCH**	**8**
SCOTTISH	**4**	**NATIVE AMERICAN**	**9**
RUSSIAN	**5**	**HUNGARIAN**	**10**

Interestingly, Michael Jordan, Michael Jackson, Denzel Washington, Oprah Winfrey and all other African American icons together do not possess a large enough percentage of America's wealth to obtain representation in this survey. The same is true for Julio Iglecias, Ricky Martin and other Hispanic American icons.

In 1 Corinthians 9:25, Apostle Paul explains that *Everyone who competes for the prize must be temperate in all things. Now they do it for a perishable crown; but we for an imperishable crown.*[26] You must be temperate to compete for the prize of wealth and success. *Webster's* defines temperate as marked by moderation, use of restraint, sobriety and self-

[26] Paraphrased 1 Corinthians 9:25

control, moderate in indulgence, not extreme or excessive.[27] You will not maintain millionaire status lacking restraint and self-control, no matter how 'lucky' you think you are. Millions require discipline. Without discipline, a fortune quickly becomes misfortune.

Webster's also defines *perishability* as the quality or condition to be destroyed, ruined, spoiled or deteriorated, to cause to die.[28] There is a possibility, though remote, that you can obtain riches from winning. But you will not sustain your gains without temperance. Your crown prize will surely perish just as many have before you.[29] Your wealth will die, spoil and deteriorate. Sadly, it will take a significant part of you away with it. Please do not put your faith in the lottery or the gaming industry. Believe in God for He promises, "*whoever believes in Him shall not perish but have everlasting life*" (*John 3:16*). We compete for a crown that will not perish.

It is fine to occasionally become a contestant on a television game show or enter a free contest. God is able to bless you by allowing you to win valuable prizes including cash. Money can come from many different sources. However, money stays and doubles and triples from the millionaire formula: more productive work, less wasteful spending, smarter sound investments and 'good old fashioned' discipline. True winners always gear up for the game. The ball is in your court. Are you ready to play?

---

[27] *Webster's New Collegiate Dictionary*
1981 G. & C. Merriam Company: Springfield, Massachusetts
[28] Ibid.
[29] Sabih, Jennifer
4/9/98 CBS 2 News Special Assignment: "After The Jackpot"

Chapter 8

Lost and Found:

Finders Keepers, Losers Weepers

"For whoever desires to save his life will lose it, but whoever loses his life for My sake will find it." Matthew 16:25

Remember the old nursery rhyme, 'Find a penny, pick it up, and all day long you'll have good luck.' Most people have experienced the thrill of finding money. No matter how small the amount, you appreciated it like a gift.

As a child, I used to pull up the cushions on our couch and dig in the upholstery of my mom's car and my dad's recliner. I was certain to find some spare coins that had been dropped from the pockets of unsuspecting individuals. Chances are the owners did not even miss their loss. However, their loss was my gain, and I loved it.

Although the seat cushion is a popular place to find money, people have found money in some unlikely venues. Many of us have heard stories: a young man out jogging finds a bag with a large sum of unmarked bills behind a dumpsite on his route. Maybe we know someone who purchased a house or a used car later finding a hidden treasure in their possession. We dream of blessed occasions like this, but they seldom happen. Finding money is actually an unpredictable and uncontrollable occurrence, even when one searches the most likely places.

We enjoy finding money, because it takes little or no effort on our part. We view it as a free gift, no strings attached. Our general attitude is: 'finders keepers, losers weepers.' We rarely take into account the predicament of the owner. She is simply the loser. Our regard to her is, 'be more careful next time.'

Our posture in this situation turns full circle when we are the losers. Imagine dropping your wallet in a movie theater and discovering that it is lost hours later. You become frantic. First, you try to trace your steps in hopes of recalling where it might be. You try to remember when you saw it last. If your quest is unsuccessful, you pick up the telephone and start canceling your credit cards. After all, not many are honest enough today to return free money to its rightful owner. We react this way because we are unsure of how others might respond to finding our money. If we were the finder, would we try to locate the owner or would we just consider it a blessing and move on?

A wallet usually contains the owner's name, identification, and in most cases address or telephone number. Making no attempt to return it would be criminal. But, what about that bag of unmarked bills behind the dumpsite or that suitcase full of cash hidden in the trunk of your new-used car, would you try to return that money also?

Hunting for hidden treasure is no foreign concept. Go to any beach site or oceanfront and you are likely to see someone scouring the sand with a metal detector. This individual is probably looking for a forgotten buried treasure, a lost valuable or anything of worth. Sometimes she finds exactly what she is looking for.

Many of our forefathers joined a victimless quest for riches also. The Gold Rush began in 1849. People packed up their belongings and trekked out westward to California in hopes of striking gold. California's population grew from about 14,000 in 1848 to approximately 380,000 in 1860.[1]

---

[1] Chidsey, D.B.
1968 The California Gold Rush: Grolier Electronic Publishing

The thought of finding enough gold dust, flakes and nuggets to retire and live lavishly was quite enticing. Unfortunately, gold mining was a long shot and a gamble, much like some of the other efforts to obtain wealth we discussed in the previous chapter.

Webster's defines *rush* as moving forward, progress, acting with haste or eagerness, without preparation, to perform in a short time or at a high unnatural speed, marked by a special urgency.[2]

There were three groups of participants in the Gold Rush. The first two of the three were miners. Most of the miners were fortunate if they found tiny particles. Discouraged by the long hours and low pay (which was nothing unless you found gold), they gave up. This first type of miners chalked up their losses to poor and impulsive career decisions. However, the second type of miner was relentless in their pursuit. They hung in there and refused to quit. Intent on defying the odds, they panned until their hands became sore.

The third group of participants in the Gold Rush were non-miners. This group of visionaries made a profit no matter what happened at the mines. These people made lemonade when others only saw lemons. Instead of spending a fortune buying pick axes, pans, dredges and the other tools of the gold rush trade, they chose to set up shop. These shrewd businessmen had the foresight to identify the needs of the miners, and they provided those necessities for profit. Their role was very similar to the role of brokerage firms of today. Investors spend hours researching stocks, bonds or mutual funds in an effort to find the winners. However, the brokerage firm makes a profit on every transaction, whether the investor strikes gold or not.

---

[2] *Webster's New Collegiate Dictionary*
1981 G. & C. Merriam Company: Springfield, Massachusetts

Searching for riches can prove to be a fruitless adventure. However, if one has the infallible source, pay dirt is easily obtained. In Matthew 17:24-27, Jesus is confronted with paying the temple tax. He gives Apostle Peter specific directions: "*Go to the sea, cast in a hook, and take the fish that comes up first. And when you have opened its mouth, you will find a piece of money" (Matthew 17:27).*

Finding money is an acceptable means of acquiring wealth. However, many people spend their entire lives searching and never finding what they desire, because they are looking for the wrong things in all the wrong places. Jesus Christ directs us to "*Seek first the kingdom of God and His righteousness, and all these things shall be added unto you*" (Matthew 6:33). Finding Christ will not disappoint you. He is more precious than silver, gold, and any priceless gem. *"The silver is Mine, and the gold is Mine, says the Lord of hosts" (Haggai 2:8).*

"For whoever desires to save his life will lose it, but who ever loses his life for My sake will find it" (Matthew 16:25).

Chapter 9

Do Not Sell Your Soul For Money

The Price Is Much Too High

For what will it profit a man if he gains the whole world, and loses his own soul? Or what will a man give in exchange for his soul?"
Mark 8:36

There are more negative methods of obtaining money than the ones we examined in the preceding chapters. Begging, borrowing and stealing are the absolute worst possible ways to acquire cash. Unfortunately, many of us have obtained money by these means. If you have not personally done so, surely you know of someone who has participated in one or more of these foul practices. This chapter is designed to disclose the pitfalls associated with these acts and to reveal God's attitude toward this behavior.

First, let us discuss begging. There are two types of begging: public and private. Both occur on a regular basis.

Begging For Mercy

Most of us have been approached by a beggar while walking along a public street, while waiting at a traffic light or when entering or exiting a store. These experiences qualify as public begging.

In chapter two, we observed the fact that every major American metropolis has a skid row. Homelessness has become an issue of increasing concern for our nation. Today, we cannot drive down a public street without seeing indigence.[*]

Many times we give money to these people, because they appear to be in such dire straits. Some of them have mental challenges. Almost all of them seem to be in need of the bare essentials: food, adequate clothing and shelter. We are blessed to be a blessing to others. Helping those in need is the right thing to do. *"Give generously to him and do so without a grudging heart; then because of this the Lord your God will bless you in all your work and in everything you put your hand to do. There will always be poor people in the land. Therefore I command you to be open-handed toward your brothers and toward the poor and needy in your land" (Deuteronomy 15:10,11)*[1]

Some of us have concerns about giving money to public beggars. Many times these individuals are addicted to drugs and or alcohol. If you believe the beggar will use your money to purchase drugs or alcohol, do not give him your money. Instead, purchase or prepare the food, clothing or other item you wish to give him on your own. Then simply give it to that individual. He should be grateful to receive your kindness.

Your gifts to the poor are considered to be alms. The term "alms" comes from the Greek word: *Eleemosune*, which means compassion exercised toward the poor, a merciful deed or charity given freely to relieve the poor.[2] It is human to pity the predicament of these poverty-stricken individuals. God honors our selfless consideration of those less fortunate.

---

[*] See Chapter Two

[1] Dueteronomy 15:11 New International Version

[2] Strong, James
1990 *Strong's Exhaustive Concordance of the Bible*: Thomas Nelson Publishers: Nashville, TN: reference 1654

Though we sympathize with the public beggar, most of us cannot identify with his lifestyle. We have no idea what it is like to be out on the streets. Where would we go, if we did not have a place to live? What would we do without any money? Sometimes helping them makes us feel better about ourselves. Observing them certainly makes us better appreciate what we have. Jesus Christ told us the poor will be with us always.[3] We may not be in a position to cure world hunger or eliminate homelessness. However, we should all do our part to help. We are held accountable for our actions and our inaction. Cannon Farrar stated it best in these words:

I am only one. But I am one.

I cannot do everything. But I can do something.

What I can do, I ought to do.

And what I ought to do, by the grace of God I will do.[4]

Begging To Be Rescued

Private begging is an entirely different issue. Where the public beggar begs for mercy and compassion, the private beggar begs to be rescued. Do you remember the story of 'The Boy Who Cried Wolf?' When he cried, the people of his town came running to rescue him from disaster, only to find him in no danger at all. He cried again and they came running.

---

[3] Paraphrased Matthew 26:11

[4] Munroe, Myles
1991 *Understanding You Potential*: Foreword by Jerry Horner: Destiny Image Publishers: Shippensburg, PA

The boy liked the idea of having people come to his rescue. He also liked the control of knowing that all he had to do was open his mouth to receive assistance. This boy practiced the art of manipulation and performed it well. However, the townspeople quickly grew tired of this routine. The third time the boy cried wolf, they did not respond. Only this time there really was a wolf and the boy got eaten alive. This young boy died before he realized that his time would have been much better spent learning to defend and protect himself against real danger, as opposed to depending on the rescue of others. Private beggars have the same mentality as 'The Boy Who Cried Wolf.' They too should be enrolled in Independence 101, the course for crybabies.

Gimme Jimmy

Most of us have experienced private begging. A relative, friend or co-worker approaches you asking, "Spare me some change, I want a snack." Your tennis partner says, "Would you give me a few dollars, I am a little short today?" Your neighbor invites you to lunch at her favorite restaurant and when the bill comes she conveniently discovers that she does not have her wallet. "I'm sorry, could you cover me this time?" she apologizes. How about that kooky cousin who only calls you when he needs a few bucks to pay his gas bill or a ride to his girlfriend's house? These are all examples of private begging and we like to call these private beggars, 'Gimme Jimmys.'

Although Gimme Jimmy behavior appears to be merely annoying on the surface, if allowed to continue, it becomes reckless disregard for others. Gimme Jimmys cry wolf. Many Gimme Jimmys feel that, those they mooch off of owe them.*

---

* See Genesis Chapter 13 Lot fought with Abraham over the wealth he obtained as a result of Abraham's blessing.

They have a multiplicity of excuses for why others should rescue them by financing their lives.

Gimme Jimmy's often develop this behavior as a result of being financial out-care patients. You might ask, "What are financial out-care patients?" Financial out-care patients are adult children (wolf crying boys and girls), who have never fully mastered adulthood.[5] They usually continue to live with their parents far beyond the age of adolescence. When or if they leave the coop, they are prone to return occasionally. In addition to relying on parents for shelter, they also tap the coffers of their parents regularly. This double whammy can be a draining experience that leaves most parents searching for answers.

No Training, No Gaining

Many parents wonder why it is so difficult for their adult children to cut the financial umbilical cord. They often blame themselves, asking, "Where did we go wrong?" Although the parents are not completely at fault, they are usually accomplices to this crime. Parents are given the huge responsibility of preparing their children for adulthood. Their job is done, when their child can stand on his or her own two feet. Sadly, sometimes this never happens. The Bible admonishes parents, *"Train up a child in the way he should go, and when he is old he will not depart from it" (Proverbs 22:6).*

I often hear pastors, ministers and others teach on this topic. While it is good, much of this teaching barely scratches the surface. In general, Proverbs 22:6 deals with teaching your children the fear and admonition of the Lord and giving

---

[5] Stanley, Thomas and Danko William Ph.Ds
1996 *The Millionaire Next Door: The Surprising Secrets of America's Wealthy*: Pocket books: New York, NY

them guidance. It makes clear that parents are to help children identify their specific gifts and callings. It is helpful, however, to consider the specific context surrounding this scripture. If we observe the verses that precede and follow, the author is specifically addressing the subject of riches. In other words, adequate training requires that parents teach their children how to manage their finances.

Could it be that parents under the guise of love are enabling their children to be financial out-care patients? Codependency extends from insecurity. Insecurity results from a failure to develop a sense of self worth. Children that are not taught financial responsibility can never become self-sufficient. The codependency issues of parents can cause the children to experience dependency problems. They are handicapped by uncertainty, lack of assurance, insecurity and instability. Parents should love their children completely and unconditionally. However, the Bible warns us that a child left to his own devices will bring his mother to shame.[6] Set your child up for success. Do not foster his failure. Do not raise a Gimme Jimmy that repeatedly cries wolf. Remember, it is never too late to change and change begins with you!

Mastering Maturity

Private beggars are not entirely faultless, after all they are adults and their loved ones do not put guns to their heads to make them take money or live with them. In I Corinthians 13:11, Apostle Paul says, "When I was a child, I spoke as a child, I understood as a child, I thought as a child: but when I became a man, I put away childish things." Some adult children must remind themselves that it is time to put away

---

[6] Paraphrased Proverbs 29:15

childish things. It is time they except responsibility for their own lives.

Lest I be too strict, I might add that there are certain instances when it is perfectly fine for an adult child to live with her parents. As a matter of fact, unmarried children are often encouraged to stay with their parents; particularly young women, because their fathers serve as their covering until they marry. Nevertheless, living at home with parents does not preclude them from carrying their share of the financial burdens of the home. Their contribution should include, but should not be limited to: paying rent, and a part of the utilities, telephone and grocery bills, also paying for their own car expenses.

We have every intention of providing a home for our children as long as necessary. However, our children will learn to maintain a budget and contribute to the upkeep of our home as long as they reside with us. This will prepare them for adulthood, marriage and the real world. This will set them up for success.

Begging is manipulation at its finest. The beggar intends to appeal to his victim's sympathetic, compassionate side. Begging is not an acceptable method of obtaining money. The beggar is clearly trying to get something free, without obligation. Sometimes begging works. People feel sorry enough for you to give you what you want. However, 'The Boy Who Cried Wolf' teaches us that desired results are random. One should never depend upon other people to provide his or her needs. In Philippians 4:19, Apostle Paul proclaims, *"And my God shall supply all your need according to His riches in glory by Christ Jesus."* True security lies in God, not others.

Begging is also very demeaning. Going to others for money makes a profound statement. The beggar is saying: "I am irresponsible. I cannot or will not take care of myself. I am really a child trapped in an adult body. Please, be my parent?" If this is not the type of message you wish to send, do not beg.

Whimpy Everywhere

When I was young, I used to love watching the Popeye cartoon. Whimpy was my favorite character on the show. Whimpy would walk into a restaurant and tell the waiter, "I will gladly pay you Tuesday for a hamburger today." As a child, I thought this scene was hilarious, because I was naive enough to believe that such a situation would never happen in real life. I thought no one could get away with that. Now that I am all grown up, I am enlightened to find Whimpys everywhere. I am sure you know them too. I always hear statements like, "Put it on my tab! "I owe you one." "Do you accept charge cards?" Needless to say, Whimpy is no longer my favorite cartoon character.

Buy Now Pay Later

Borrowing is another very negative method of obtaining money. However, many people are in debt up to their eyeballs. Borrowing is a very deceptive practice. When you borrow, you are essentially mortgaging your future. The problem is, no one really knows what will happen from one day to the next. Thus, you made a promise you may be unable to keep. The Bible warns us, "*Boast not for tomorrow, for no man knows what the future holds.*"[7]

I often wonder why people borrow money. Why would anyone in their right mind choose a lifestyle of indebtedness? I am convinced that there is a spirit of lust

---

[7] Paraphrased Proverbs 27:1

behind borrowing. Something inside an individual tells him, 'I need this now and I cannot wait until I have the money to purchase it.' He is driven by his desires, and he lacks restraint.

The good thing about borrowing (if there is any good in borrowing), is borrowing buys you some time. Unfortunately, it costs you much more. It costs you your freedom. Proverbs 22:7 states, "The borrower is servant to the lender." A servant is a slave. I do not know many people who would agree to being enslaved. Yet, I do know many people who are deep in debt.

Borrow and Tomorrow Can Bring Sorrow

In 2 Kings 4:1,2 we witness the result of the attempt made by the widow's husband to buy time. I am certain he thought he would be able to repay his debt. I am also certain he thought he would live to see tomorrow, and everything would go according to his plan. However, things do not always go according to our plan. I am sure, as a God-fearing man, he never intended to jeopardize the well being of his family. Nevertheless, that is exactly what he did.

The scripture does not explain how he died, but my sanctified imagination tells me his debt probably had something to do with it. 2 Kings was written between the years 560 B.C. and 538 B.C. During this time, contractual relationships were often established with the intent of allowing a man to borrow to the point where he was unable to repay his debt. Then, this man would be forced into a life of servitude to his lender. People often worked themselves to death without repaying their debt in full. Adversely, the unforgiving lender still expected to be paid. Ultimately, the heirs of the indebted person became responsible for making good on the loan. It is evident that this cycle could continue for generations. This situation may sound foreign at first blush, but let us bring it up to modern terms.

Buying or borrowing time may sound like a win- win situation. The lender is happy, because he is compensated with interest, usually. The borrower is also happy, because he gets what he wants today and he can pay for it over a period of time instead of all at once. Notwithstanding, the borrower probably does not take into consideration the time value of money and the power of compound interest.

Because we live in an inflationary society, we expect our personal wealth to increase as a result of how we invest our resources. If I provide you a good or service for which you cannot pay cash, I expect to be given additional compensation for extending credit to you. Each day that goes by that you do not completely pay off your debt, the amount of your debt increases due to the interest I charge you. Credit card companies, mortgage bankers and others in the money lending business understand the time value of money and the power of compound interest. It is their business to understand.

Much like the lenders of old, today's lenders will do anything and everything to get people to take on as much debt as they can possibly stand. Actually, they encourage you take on more than you can stand. Remember what I said about the biblical lender? Well, it still applies. Lenders will never tell you to stop borrowing. Lenders will never tell you "slow down and truly consider the costs versus the benefit of making one more purchase," because they do not care one bit about your welfare. Their job is to sell credit as long as you are willing to buy it!

We have already established the fact that lenders do not encourage you to exercise self-control. Yet if you become overburdened, due to your lack of restraint, they harass you by mail and by phone. Eventually they will repossess all of your goods, foreclose on your home, and if necessary, force you into bankruptcy! What wonderful people lenders are.

Borrowing is a very negative and unproductive method of obtaining money. The costs outweigh the benefits. Do not be deceived. Contrary to popular belief, you do not need it today. Do not buy the lie. Wait until you can afford it. Do not become a Whimpy. Do not borrow! *"You shall lend to many nations, but you shall not borrow" (Deuteronomy 28:12).*

Here we give you a cursory examination of borrowing. For a more comprehensive strategy of eradicating debt and reclaiming control of your financial future, read book two of our trilogy: Escape From Debtors Prison entitled, *LET MY PEOPLE GO!*

Thou Shalt Not Steal

Most people know that stealing is a criminal offense punishable by law. However, robbery, car theft, burglary and embezzlement are not the only ways that people steal. *Webster's* defines stealing as taking something without permission or authorization, taking anything that is not rightfully yours and this includes fraudulent or questionable behavior.[8] Unfortunately, people steal all the time. In many cases, they do this throughout their entire lives without understanding the ramifications of what they have done.

One can observe a young toddler or infant taking an object off his mother's dresser or his father's desk as soon as he is physically capable of doing so. Most adults realize that young children are exceptionally curious, so they typically encourage and nurture children through their exploratory stages. However, many parents face great difficulty

---

[8] *Webster's New Collegiate Dictionary*
1981 G. & C. Merriam Company: Springfield, Massachusetts

disciplining and directing their children away from potentially dangerous objects. One might often view a parent following her young toddler or infant all around the house, taking the things that may hurt him out of reach or out of sight. The words, "no" and "don't" mean absolutely nothing to a child this age.

No matter how much they adore us, our parents cannot continue to follow us around conveniently removing temptation from our reach or out of our sight. At some point, we are on our own. We then have to distinguish right from wrong for ourselves.

When a young adult graduates from high school or college she is told, "The world is your oyster." She realizes that she is at a stage where her whole life is in front of her. The proud graduate is very anxious to take the world by storm. It is possible, however, that no one explained to her that hard work and integrity are the keys to doing so. Regrettably, if she did not learn this important lesson, she is doomed to make some vital mistakes.

Manipulative Manny

Webster's defines *manipulation*, to control or play upon by artful, unfair, or insidious means especially to one's own advantage; also to change by artful or unfair means so as to serve one's purpose.[9] Manipulation is a widely used form of stealing, because the manipulator takes what does not rightfully belong to him.

There are adults who have not out-grown the mentality of their infant and toddler years. "No" and "don't" still mean absolutely nothing to them. We call these types of people Manipulative Mannys. Here is the standard abbreviated life

---

[9] *Webster's New Collegiate Dictionary*
1981 G. & C. Merriam Company: Springfield, Massachusetts

story of Manipulative Manny, categorized by each major life stage.

Infancy:	Manny begins to walk and pull down objects from the kitchen table.
Toddler:	Manny takes his mother's hair clips and buries them in a house plant.
Preschool:	Manny takes cookies from the cookie jar. But when his dad questions him, Manny denies it.
Grade School:	Manny learns to copy answers from his friend's paper.
Junior High:	Manny starts making cheat sheets of his own.
High School:	Manny plagiarizes his book report.
College:	Manny obtains a copy of the test and starts dating his roommate's girlfriend.
Grad. School:	Manny has someone else write his final paper.

1st Job:	Manny embellishes his credentials, lies about his previous work experience and uses his relatives as references in order to get the job.
1st Wife:	Manny marries his high school sweetheart after getting her pregnant.
Work:	Manny spends most of his time completing personal tasks at work and cheats on his income taxes.
Extra-marital:	Manny has an affair with his secretary.
Promotion:	Manny gets promoted by taking credit for his assistant's work.
Management:	Manny begins to embezzle funds from the company.

Manipulative Manny's title might be Division Manager, but his job description should read thief. Although the company name is on his paycheck, Manny works for the devil. "*The thief does not come except to steal, and to kill and to destroy" (John 10:10).* Manny is Satan's employee. It's a pity that he doesn't even know it.

The life story of Manipulative Manny parallels that of many people today. What started out as cute, mischievous, juvenile behavior has snowballed into criminal conduct. The truth is this conduct was always criminal. As little tikes we started to take things that did not belong to us. We continued to do the same as we grew up. Later, we still keep taking until we cannot take anymore. Why did not someone sit us down and explain to us that the world was not our oyster. Everything is not ours for the taking. Some things should be off limits.

Please understand that nobody gets away with anything. Even if others never discover your dishonesty, God knows the truth. He sees everything and He is sovereign. Justice will come in time. In Galatians 6:7, Apostle Paul states, *"Do not be deceived. God is not mocked. For whatever a man sows, that he shall also reap."* Besides, the harvest is always bigger than the seed. Whatever you decide to do, like a boomerang, it will return right back to you. Beware of the fact that your wrong-doing comes back much worse than it went out.

David, King of Israel learned this the hard way. An incident of voyeurism spun its way into a web of lies, deception and ultimately murder. One spring night, David woke up and went out on the roof of his castle. While he was out there, he saw a beautiful woman bathing. King David found the woman to be very attractive. He asked around and learned that her name was Bathsheba, and she was the wife of a soldier in his army named Uriah.

King David had an affair with Bathsheba, and she conceived his child. First he tried to cover up his crime by granting Uriah a weekend pass to go home and sleep with his wife. Uriah returned to Jerusalem but he did not go down to his own house. Uriah did not think it would be fair for him to enjoy the comfort of his home, while his fellow soldiers were still encamped in the open fields for combat.

After David's cover-up attempt did not work, he told the captain of the army to send Uriah out in the forefront of the hottest battle, and leave him there so he would be killed. The captain obeyed the king, and Uriah was murdered. When Bathsheba heard what happened to Uriah, she mourned the death of her husband. Later, King David brought her to his castle, married her, and she bore him a son.

It appeared that King David had managed to save face with his people by keeping his extra-marital affair with Bathsheba a secret. But, the Lord cursed David for his vicious acts saying, *"Behold, I will raise up adversity against you from your own house; and I will take your wives before your eyes and give them to your neighbor, and he shall lie with your wives in the sight of the sun. For you did it secretly, but I will do this thing before all Israel, before the sun...Because by this deed you have given great occasion to the enemies of the Lord to blaspheme, the child also who is born to you shall surely die" (2 Samuel 12:14).* What is done in the dark shall be revealed in the light. No one gets away with murder. Evil deeds do not go unpunished.

King David was not a Manipulative Manny in the purest sense of the example, because manipulation did not characterize his entire life. As we mentioned in Chapter 5, David was a man after God's own heart. King David's error shows that even sincere Christians need to beware of the lure of manipulation.

As Christians we should be careful not to let the Manipulative Manny's of this world rattle us. The Lord says, "*Vengeance is mine and I shall repay.*"[10] We walk around angry and frustrated about what Manipulative Manny has done, when we are supposed to know that God is in control.

[10] Paraphrased Romans 12:19

If we truly believe that the Almighty God has this and every matter covered, then why do we try to fix things ourselves? The battle is not yours. It is the Lord's. Again Apostle Paul encourages us in Romans 8:31: *"If God is for us, who can be against us?"*[11]

Manipulation is the same as stealing. People take things that do not rightfully belong to them all the time. You may not be as bad as Manipulative Manny or King David. However, you should not diminish the impact of that little white lie you told, because you did not want to hurt someone's feelings; or that personal time you took when you were on the clock and there was work to be done. Perhaps the cashier gave you too much change from your purchase and you decided take it and not to say anything; or your baby walked out of the store with some candy that you did not pay for and you elected not to return, because you were too embarrassed. Maybe the phone rang and you did not want to talk to the caller, so you had your wife say that you were not at home. All these things qualify as lies, deception, manipulation, cheating and stealing. In Exodus 20:15, the Lord commanded, "*Thou shalt not steal.*"

It is a good thing we have the redemptive power of Christ on our side. All we have to do is ask forgiveness. *"If we confess our sins, He is faithful and just to forgive us our sins and to cleanse us from all unrighteousness. If we say that we have not sinned, we make him a liar, and His word is not in us" (1 John 1:9,10).*

Do not get trapped in this downward spiral to the toilet. Satan has enough people working for him. Do not join forces with the enemy. He cannot offer you any benefits, because God has all of the benefits. *"Bless the Lord, O my soul and forget not all his benefits" (Psalm 103:2).*

---

[11] Romans 8:31 New International Version

Do not resort to begging, borrowing or stealing. They are the worse possible methods of obtaining money. Do not sell your soul for money. The price is much too high. *"For what will it profit a man if he gains the whole world, and loses his own soul? Or what will a man give in exchange for his soul" (Mark 8:36).*

Chapter 10

Money Does Grow On Trees

Whatever a man sows, that he will also reap. Galatians 6:7

The best method of obtaining money is by growing it. I can hear my mother's sweet southern voice saying, "Baby, money don't grow on trees." I disagree with those well-intending mothers around the world. I grow money. In Galatians 6:7, Apostle Paul tells us, "Whatever a man sows, that he will also reap." It is time we introduce you to a new concept, one your mother probably did not know anything about. This chapter discusses a concept we refer to as "financial farming."

Everyone knows that it takes money to make money. Since the Bible does not advocate indebtedness, it is best to start with your own money.* In order to grow, you must first sow. Growing money begins with debt elimination and saving. We addressed the trials associated with debt in the prior chapter.* Here, we will consider saving money.

Earning money represents you working for money. However, growing money represents money working for you. Although working for money is a noble endeavor, you achieve financial security by having your money work for you. Subsequently, when your money works hard, you do not have to. Be mindful of the fact that your job is not your source. Your job is only a resource, a place to obtain seed to grow your wealth.

---

* Scope of this book does not cover complex investment vehicles like partnerships or corporations which provide debt-free growth outlets.

* See book two of our trilogy: Escape From Debtors Prison, *Let My People Go!* for a complete debt elimination strategy.

I believe the Beatles said it best with their popular hit in the 60's, "Money Can't Buy Me Love." Although money cannot buy love or happiness, it does buy options. Options represent the ability to choose from a variety of alternatives. Options equal freedom. They give you the power to decide what your future holds. You get to design your own life.

Do you want a life dictated by poor planning and circumstances? Or would you like to determine your quality of life? The choice is yours. You determine whether you live, survive or just exist. Make a decision to live your life on purpose, not just barely getting by. Take control. Become a financial farmer.

Tough Job, But Somebody Has To Do It

The financial farmer treats sowing money seed as his occupation. He is not simply a person who incidentally sows financial seed, but he is a "sower." Sowing money seed is not an option, it is his livelihood.

Poverty is a curse. *"The destruction of the poor is their poverty" (Proverbs 10:15). Jesus said, I came to preach the gospel to the poor.*[1] A financial farmer sows seed to break the curse of poverty and to exhibit the good news to the economically impoverished. That good news is: You do not have to be poor anymore, if you become a sower!

Financial farming is not easy, because it requires discipline. The financial farmer must sow, even when he does not feel like sowing. *"Those who sow in tears shall reap in joy"* (Psalm 126:5). Our pastor, Bishop Charles E. Blake preached a sermon that addressed this topic. He entitled this sermon, "Weeping Before Reaping." Bishop Blake explained how the farmer makes the tough decision to delay

[1] Paraphrased Luke 4:18

gratification. The farmer knows that he cannot eat (or spend) his seed today and expect a harvest later. A financial farmer saves so that he will have more seed to sow.

Ecclesiastes 3:1-2 states, "*To everything there is a season, and a time for every purpose under heaven...A time to plant and a time to pluck what has been planted.*"[2] Financial farmers understand the seasons, because they know how God operates. After the flood, God cut a covenant with creation. He promised, "*While the earth remains, seedtime and harvest, cold and heat, winter and summer, and day and night shall not cease*" (*Genesis 8:22).* Since everything that God promised continues without fail, the financial farmer is confident that if he plants during seedtime, his harvest will surely come.

The law of progression requires the financial farmer to be patient. In Mark 4:26-29, Jesus illustrates the law of progression in his 'Parable of the Growing Seed.'

"The kingdom of God is as if a man should scatter seed on the ground, and should sleep by night and rise by day, and the seed should sprout and grow, he himself does not know how. For the earth yields crops by itself: first the blade, then the head, after that the full grain in the head. But when the grain ripens, immediately he puts in the sickle, because the harvest has come."[3]

Dr. Creflo Dollar, pastor of World Changers Church International, College Park, Georgia, said it best, "You can't plant seed today and eat collard greens tomorrow. It takes time." Any experienced financial farmer realizes this. He does not pick fruit from the tree prematurely. He nurtures his harvest to maturity, and protects it from the elements. The financial farmer does not put his money into a 90-day certificate of deposit at his local bank on Monday and go back

---

[2] Paraphrased Ecclesiastes 3:1,2

[3] Mark 4:26-29 New King James Version

to withdraw it on Friday. He knows there will be substantial penalties for early withdrawal. Instead, he stays in it for the long haul. He looks forward to reaping a bountiful and ripe harvest!

A good financial farmer sows many seeds. He does not pinch pennies during his planting. After all, he is sowing toward a sound financial future. In 2 Corinthians 9:6, Apostle Paul explains, "*He who sows sparingly will also reap sparingly, and he who sows bountifully will also reap bountifully.*" This is a wonderful passage of scripture. It is not focused solely on reaping a large harvest for yourself. The word bountifully comes from the Greek word *Eulogia*, meaning with blessings. This relates to the sower giving to others; and as a result of his generosity the sower is blessed along with the recipient of his gift.

This type of sowing may not make sense to the natural mind. Getting more money by giving more money defies logic. However, Luke proclaims, *"It is more blessed to give than to receive" (Acts 20:35).* God blesses us to be a blessing to others. He told Abraham, the father of our faith, *Through you shall all people on the earth be blessed.*[4]

Grounds For Consideration

A good farmer understands that, where he plants is just as important as what, when and how much he plants. He knows the quality of the ground in which he sows will have a profound effect on the quality of his harvest.

A good farmer knows he must sow in good ground. Good ground is fertile soil. *Webster's* defines *fertile* as producing or bearing fruit in great quantities, productive, plentiful, capable of sustaining abundant plant growth,

[4] Paraphrased Genesis 12:2,3

affording abundant possibilities for development, capable of producing fruit, capable of growing or developing, and having the power to reproduce in kind or to assist in reproduction and growth.[5] Fertile soil is rich in nutrients. It is capable of supporting and producing fruit.

In Matthew 13, we find the Parable of the Sower. Here Jesus chronicles a day in the life of a sower. We find that the sower sows in four different types of ground. However, only one type of ground yields a successful harvest, the good ground.

In verses eighteen through twenty-three, Jesus explains the reasons for crop failure in three distinct cases and the formula for success in the final scenario. Clearly, this parable is not about money. Nonetheless, we can draw several financial lessons from this text.

In the first instance, the seeds fall by the wayside and the birds come and eat them. This is a classic case of trusting someone who is financially inept with your hard earned money. In Matthew 7:6, Jesus warns, "Do not give what is holy to the dogs; nor cast your pearls before swine, lest they trample them under their feet, and turn and tear you in pieces." This mistake can prove to be fatal, as it may leave you in financial ruin. You should always verify the experience, reputation and wisdom of those in whom you trust to manage your finances.

In the second instance, the seed falls on stony ground where there is little earth. This represents an individual who possesses some technical skills, but is not very experienced. When hardship or challenges come, he responds with immaturity. This response usually leads to unnecessary mistakes. A great example of this would be a stockbroker who is fresh out of college. A brokerage firm hires him, and assigns your account to him. The first time the stock market

---

[5] *Webster's New Collegiate Dictionary*
1981 G. & C. Merriam Company: Springfield, Massachusetts

drops 100 points, he panics and sells half of your portfolio, moving your funds into a money market account. The next day the market rises a hundred and fifty points. You just lost $10,000 in less than 24 hours. The inexperienced novice can cost you big bucks.

In the third instance, the seed falls among thorns. A good example of this case would be the Registered Investment Advisor or Certified Financial Planner. This individual may be experienced, but he is also rather arrogant and greedy. He becomes very busy bragging about how he bagged "the big one," because your account is worth millions. He also becomes so preoccupied with calculating how he will spend his fat commission checks, that his attention is diverted from watching your nest egg. Distraction and egotism render him virtually useless to you. You must sever ties with this gentleman quickly, before he loses the whole farm!

In the fourth and final instance, the successful farmer sows in good ground, because he knows exactly what it takes to prosper. He does not waste his time or his money investing in hair-brained, get-rich-quick schemes. He ignores the advice he overheard at the water cooler. He does not let all of his seed ride on the latest craze (at the time of this writing that would be 'dot com' investments). Instead, the successful farmer invests consistently over time, knowing he will eventually reap his harvest. He does not lose his patience and waste precious energy worrying. He understands what Apostle Paul meant when he encouraged us in Galatians 6:9 saying, *Do not grow weary in well doing: for in due season you shall reap, if you faint not.*[6] He also realizes that over-anxious activity would be counter-productive. *"Do not wear yourself out to get rich; have the wisdom to show restraint" (Proverbs 23:4).*[7] Sowing in good ground is investing wisely

[6] Paraphrased Galatians 6:9

[7] Proverbs 23:4 New International Version

and regularly. Always consider the ground in which you plant. It can have a huge impact on your harvest.

Making Wise Decisions

Now that we comprehend what it means to grow money, let us turn our attention to the different methods of achieving this goal.

Proverbs is the biblical book of wisdom. It is good to seek the assistance of those who are savvy in the area of investments. *"Whoever loves instruction loves knowledge, but he who hates correction is stupid" (Proverbs 12:1)* Also, Proverbs 3:5 exhorts us to trust God and lean not to our own understanding.[8] Additionally, we are encouraged to, *"Get wisdom! Get understanding! ... Wisdom is the principal thing; therefore, get wisdom. And in all your getting, get understanding" (Proverbs 4:5,7).*

Let us make some distinctions at this point. Knowledge is the awareness of the facts. Understanding is knowing how to apply the facts. Wisdom is the actual application of the facts to your particular situation for your benefit. Thus, knowledge is required to obtain understanding, and both knowledge and understanding are needed to acquire wisdom. One must possess all three, knowledge, understanding and wisdom, in order to make wise and informed investment decisions.

We are ultimately responsible for our own well-being. Therefore, we should take time to educate ourselves about the investment vehicles we choose. One must never invest in anything he does not fully understand. If it sounds too complicated, it probably is!

---

[8] Paraphrased Proverbs 3:5

To determine the best type of investment vehicle for you, consider three things: your risk tolerance, expected rate of return on the investment and when you plan to use it. You may wonder why I use the term "vehicle" in reference to investments. I term the process this way because, investments are designed to help individuals get somewhere. That "somewhere" is your financial destination or goal. The aforementioned questions help you determine your best mode of transportation. Just as you cannot use a skateboard to get to the moon, it would not be wise to try to fund your two-year-old's college education with a savings account. We should choose the most effective plan of action to achieve our goals.

Risky Business

Risk tolerance is defined as the level of risk an investor is willing to accept in maintaining a given investment position. Each investor's risk tolerance is different. Although risk tolerance varies according to the individual investor, there are three general levels of risk. The categories are: low, medium and high risk tolerance. The following quiz will help you identify your personal risk tolerance level.

Assumption: You have $25,000 to invest.

1. Would you be able to sleep at night if the value of your investment decreased by $1,250 overnight? (5%)

2. Would you be able to sleep at night if the value of your investment decreased by $2,500 overnight? (10%)

3. Would you be able to sleep at night if the value of your investment decreased by $3,750 overnight? (15%)

If you answered no to question number one, your risk tolerance is probably low. Investment vehicles with medium or high risk factors, would not be your cup of tea. This would probably preclude you from investing in the stock market, which experiences volatility on a daily basis. However, savings accounts, money market accounts, bonds and possibly even real estate carry little or no risk. Therefore, these investment vehicles are more suited to your comfort level.

If you answered yes to number one but no to number two, your risk tolerance is probably medium. This means you are open to moderate levels of risk. There are a few more investment options available to you. In addition to low risk tolerance investments, you may consider mutual funds and blue-chip stocks of well-established corporations. Blue-chip companies have a track record of increased earnings and dividends. These investments provide the benefit of higher growth potential with a corresponding increase in potential risk.

If you answered yes to questions one and two but no to number three, your risk level is probably high (but you are no bungee jumper!) Since you are open to a higher level of risk, your investment options increase accordingly. In addition to all the investment options mentioned, you may consider medium and small cap stocks. These are medium-sized or smaller corporations that are not tried and true like the blue-chips. They are not quite as stable as larger corporations, and they probably do not provide dividends. Smaller corporations are concerned with growth. Similarly, if you desire maximum appreciation of the value of your stock shares, these small caps are most likely your best choice.

Great Expectations

The level of risk generally associated with an investment normally corresponds to the amount of return an investor can expect. Unfortunately, "People expect higher returns than they should for their particular risk level. Risk and return tend to be closely related. In general, the greater the prospect for high returns, the greater the likelihood of loss."[9] In essence, lower risk garners a lower return, and higher risk garners a higher return.

Your return expectations are vital in choosing the type of investment you need. An investor must be willing to accept higher levels of risk, if he has high return expectations. When you consider your return expectations in conjunction with your risk tolerance, you can determine your best course of investment action.

Time: Friend or Foe

When you plan on using the invested funds is just as important as the investment vehicle you choose. If you intend to use the funds in the near future, let us say for a vacation this summer, you cannot afford to invest in anything risky. The reason is that, you do not have much time to make up for fluctuations in the return on your investment, nor do you have time to make up for the risk of loss of your investment. You should play it safe. A money market account or certificate of deposit would serve your purpose well. Consider opening an

---

[9] Skakunn,Brett
1997 "Separating Fact From Folklore About Individual Investors" Oncourse Fourth Quarter Issue: Smith Barney's Consulting Group

account with one of the banks on the internet. These branchless (virtual) banks, usually offer higher interest rates on their savings and checking accounts. Additionally, some offer customers free checking accounts.

On the other hand, if you are investing the funds for a twenty-fifth wedding anniversary gift for your spouse, and the big day is four years away, you can afford to invest in something a bit more risky. This is due to the fact that you have more time to compensate for fluctuations in the return on your investment. You might consider bonds or mutual funds. You can also expect to reap higher rates of return on average, as a result of your willingness to assume more risk.

Finally, if you are investing to fund your retirement, and you expect to work at least twenty more years, you can invest in blue chip, mid-cap or small-cap stocks. A more extensive window of opportunity to invest is available. You can afford to be much more aggressive with your investment choices, because you will not need these funds for a long time. There is time to recover from any volatility in the stock market. Once again, your rate of return should be commensurate with the level of risk you take on.

Be Safe Not Sorry

Let us assume that your risk tolerance, return expectations and time horizon all allow you to invest in the stock market. You should invest wisely. Wise investing in the stock market includes diversification. Simply stated, diversification is 'not putting all your eggs in one basket.' Stocks are grouped according to the area of the economy with which they relate. These areas are referred to as sectors. Diversification is the process of investing in stocks of different sectors. This is a very wise investment strategy, because sector performance varies. When pharmaceutical companies perform well, financial corporations may not. When financial corporations do well, technology corporations may not. Diversification protects you from the risk associated with being too heavily invested in any one segment of the market.

Along this same line of logic, it is unwise to have a large percentage of your portfolio in any one stock. That is like having one really big egg in your basket. It could crack at any given time, leaving you empty handed.

Things Aren't Always What They Seem

Many people with low risk tolerance automatically assume that investing in the stock market is too risky. They believe that investing in the stock market will increase their exposure to the possible loss of their investment. This is not always true. Case studies have proven that investing a portion of your funds in the stock market can actually reduce the overall risk to your investment portfolio.

Smith Barney Inc. Consulting Group issued a report in May of 1997 that covered the investment period December 31, 1956 - December 31, 1996.[10] The results of this study were astounding. If an individual had invested 50% of his portfolio in U.S. stocks and 50% in U.S. bonds he would have earned nearly 2.5% more per year than if he had invested all of his portfolio in U.S. bonds. Surprisingly, the amount of risk he would have been exposed to was the same in both cases.[*] Also shocking is the fact that this increase in return of nearly 2.5% per year over the 40-year period would have more than doubled the value of the investor's portfolio!

---

[10] Smith Barney Consulting, Inc. A Member Of Travelers Group 1997 "Investment Diversification Using Asset Allocation: What Investors Must consider to Create Their Optimal Portfolio"

[*] This research was done in conjunction with Ibbotson Associates

Power Outage

Having a savings account is an important part of any investment strategy. However, your savings account should not be your only investment vehicle. One must invest in something other than just a savings account in order to effectively grow his or her money.

Bank of America, a conventional bank, offered a savings account that yielded a 1.01% return on the investment dollar as of April 30, 2000. Unfortunately, 1926-1998 inflation averaged 3.08%.[11] Obviously, inflation ate up any gain the savings account holder would have experienced. Additionally, the individual has to pay income taxes on the interest income he or she received. Consequently, other investment vehicles are needed to assist the investor's fight to outpace inflation. If you do not obtain other investments, you will experience a loss of purchasing power. Review our extensive discussion in chapter one on poor Ms. Margaret Moody, who fell prey to the loss of purchasing power.

Have you gone shopping lately? Did you notice how much less you get for $100 than you used to? In the past twenty years the cost of living has approximately doubled. This represents a loss of purchase power.

As a financial farmer you must not only preserve your resources, you must see to it that they grow! According to research conducted by Ibbotson Associates in 1998, on average government bonds outpaced inflation by 1.8% annually, and common stocks outpaced inflation by 8.8% annually.[*] Therefore, a prudent investor should seriously examine all of the appropriate investment vehicles we have discussed herein, and look for book three of our "Escape From

---

[11] Ibbotson Associates
1999 Chicago, Illinois

[*] Research covers 1951-1997.

Debtors Prison" trilogy entitled, *Rise Up And Possess*. In *Rise Up And Possess*, we provide a more detailed and technical analysis of investing. This book will complete your investment education, and propel you into your promise land.

Consider what kind of financial farmer you are. Do you have a tough time delaying gratification? Are you spending all of your seed? Are you settling for less, instead of waiting for the best? Or, are you sowing in tears in order to reap in joy? Maybe you are crying over crop failure, because of your poor financial farming techniques. Of course, the choice is yours. Remember that Jesus cursed the fig tree that bore no fruit.[12] Will your money tree be found barren? Or will you be blessed, because it bears much fruit?

"*Then God blessed them, and God said to them, 'Be fruitful and multiply; fill the earth and subdue it'" (Genesis 1:28).* Change your occupation to sower today.

[12] Mark 11:14

Chapter 11

The Mystery Of Money

Easy Come Easy Go

You have moved my soul far from peace;
I have forgotten prosperity. Lamentations 3:17

Joan Alexander[*] sought POTTS, International for a financial coaching session. She marched in our office exasperated, with a look of sheer frustration on her face. Obviously at her wits end, she said, "I have no idea where my money is going. I earn a decent salary, so I don't understand why my paycheck seems to mysteriously disappear every two weeks." Then she concluded, "We are a two income family, we should not be living from paycheck to paycheck."

Joan desperately wanted our help. We really wanted to help our sister in Christ. However, we needed to gather more information about Joan that would enable us to render some assistance. Rachelle traced Joan's history back approximately ten years and found something very interesting. Joan developed the same pattern as many of our other clients. She developed what we refer to as *the magic number syndrome*.

---

[*] Pseudonym: We never violate the confidentiality of any client. Case examples are combined records of several persons. Details, names, occupations and genders have been changed.

Praying For A Magic Number

In January 1990, Joan is in her last semester of college. She used student loans to finance her college education. With graduation right around the corner, Joan realizes that she needs to find a job and fast. So, she begins to pray:

> Lord,
>
> If I could just get a job making $50,000, I would be set. I would then have enough money to pay my student loans, live in a nice neighborhood, upgrade my car and live comfortably. God, please grant my prayer.

Approximately six weeks before graduation, a company offers Joan $30,000 ($35,000 actually when you include the benefits). Joan prays again:

> Well Lord,
>
> The money is not exactly what I wanted. You must be still working on my $50,000 job. But I guess everybody has to start somewhere. At least the company presents opportunities for advancement. I think I will accept this job offer. Besides, some of my class-mates have not received any offers.

After working for the company a few years, Joan is promoted twice and completes her masters degree. Her annual salary leaps to a whopping $47,000. She decides to revise her prayer request:

> Lord,
>
> I have grown to realize that $50,000 dollars a year is not enough for me to make ends meet. I need my salary to increase to at least $75,000 in order that I may live comfortably. I have worked hard, and I believe I deserve better. God, please grant my prayer.

By the time Joan walked into our office, she was clearing a net income in excess of $100,000. Unfortunately, that too was not enough. I believe that God sent Joan to POTTS, International. He does answer prayers, and she definitely needed major help.

Joan is not alone in her dilemma. Many people work and earn high wages, only to find that they have not learned how to hold on to any of their earnings. Consequently, they work harder, and earn more money, finding themselves in the same predicament. They strive for higher income goals, but the more they earn the more they spend. We were faced with the task of explaining to Joan, that more income would not solve her problem.

Joan demonstrated several problems, all of which are relatively commonplace:

1. Joan was not faithful in her tithing

2. Joan was a compulsive shopper

3. Joan had an excessive amount of revolving debt

4. Joan maintained no reserves

5. Joan did no financial farming

6. Joan did not maintain a budget

Cursed With A Curse

Although Joan is Christian, she is an immature Christian. Joan needed to accept the fact that, she was just a manager of the things she possessed and not the owner. *"The earth is the Lord's, and all its fullness, the world and those who dwell therein" (Psalm 24:1).* Joan had never come to the point where she trusted God to supply all of her needs according to His riches in glory by Christ Jesus.[1] She did not remember that it was God who answered her prayers and was responsible for the favor she received in her career. *"For promotion cometh neither from the east, nor from the west, nor from the south. But God is the judge: he putteth down one, and setteth up another"*[2] *"For it is the Lord thy God, Who teaches you to profit" (Isaiah 48:17).*

As the result of her amnesia, Joan became a victim of the curse. Joan failed to honor God by giving at least 10% of her income to support the House of God and His work. Malachi 3: 8-11 reads, *"Yet you have robbed Me!... In tithes*

---

[1] Paraphrased Philippians 4:19

[2] Psalms 75:6 King James Version

and offerings. You are cursed with a curse... Bring all the tithes into the storehouse, That there may be food in My house, And try Me now in this,... If I will not open for you the windows of heaven And pour out for you such blessing That there will not be room enough to receive it. And I will rebuke the devourer for your sakes." Joan's unwillingness to submit to God's commandment gave the devil free reign in her life, and he did what he does best, devour!

A closed-fist mentality will leave you cut off. Observe: Place a penny in the palm of your hand. Now, close your fist as tightly as you possibly can. That penny is safe and secure, it is not going anywhere? You do not have to worry about dropping it or losing it. Keep in mind that your complaint is that you do not have enough. As long as your fist is closed, however, you cannot add a dime, a nickel, a quarter or anything else to that one penny. You have left no room for growth. God truly loves you, but you must provide Him a way into your situation. How will any growth come into a closed fist? If you want more money in your hand, you must open your hand. "*Those who try to make their life secure will lose it, but those who lose their life shall preserve it.*"[3]

Joan's disobedience caused her to be at odds with God. Although she prayed, she still did not develop a close relationship with Him. She began to seek peace in material things. Jane developed a compulsive shopping habit. The more she bought, the more she wanted. Her appetite for new things became insatiable. She began to shop for no apparent reason. Jane had an enormous line of credit, largely due to her six-figure income.

Joan was living in denial. She was able to deny her problem for quite some time, because every time she maxed out one credit card, another would come in the mail. Joan's

[3] Luke 17:33 New Revised Standard Version

situation had gone beyond her control. Before she knew it, she was spending more than her take-home pay each month.

Joan started her professional career in debt. Subsequently, she neglected to devise a savings plan. Within a few months of getting her first job, Joan began to live paycheck to paycheck. Barely surviving, she never saw the value of saving for a rainy day. When emergencies came up (as they often do), she was unprepared. Joan always had a credit card to fall back on, and this became her only safety net. God forbid that Joan should lose her job, because unemployment income would not even begin to put a dent in Joan's mountain of monthly debt.

All three of Joan's employment positions had retirement plans. The employer would match up to 5% of each employee's contribution to his or her retirement account. However, Joan saw no value in saving for the future. Her motto was, "Why save for tomorrow what you could spend today." Besides, her shopping habits, student loans, house and car note, prevented her from saving anything. Joan believed that she could not afford to invest toward a sound future; her present was on shaky ground.

Working For Freedom

Last chapter we extensively discussed the importance and necessity of growing money. If you have not planted at least some money in good soil, how can you expect to reap a financial harvest? Joan must first learn how to become a sower. Otherwise, she has no right to expect a return of any amount.

Many Christians suffer with the same issues. We prayerfully ask God for help. We want Him to divinely deliver us from all our financial struggles. Yet, we do not give Him anything to work with. Perhaps we expect to walk outside and it will start raining dollar bills on our heads. Not that God cannot do this (because there is absolutely nothing He cannot do), but God probably would not do this for a non-sower.

We explained earlier that this system of receiving based on giving defies conventional wisdom. Yet, it works without fail. Abraham's grandson, Jacob understood this principle well and he demonstrated wisdom (see Genesis 30 and 31).

Jacob worked for and lived with his father in law, Laban more than fourteen years. When he was finally ready to move away and establish his own domain, Laban protested. Laban knew that Jacob had God's blessing, so he would not allow him to leave. Jacob asked Laban to give him a small portion of his herd, (every speckled, black and spotted animal) that he might start a savings for his family. Laban agreed, because Jacob did not ask for much; such a small amount could never support Jacob's very large family. Laban knew that Jacob would be forced to remain there and continue working for him.[4]

Jacob had his sons separate the few animals given to him by Laban. Meanwhile, he cared for Laban's herd, because he did not possess enough to obtain his independence.[5]

Jacob made rods of poplar and almond and chestnut trees, and peeled white streaks in them, exposing the white of the rods. He set the rods that he peeled in front of Laban's flocks where they bred. And when they came to drink, Laban's flocks bred in front of the rods and produced young that were speckled and spotted. Consequently, Jacob's flocks multiplied greatly and he became very rich.[6]

God gave Jacob the vision of owning a multitude of livestock. Jacob knew that Laban prospered because of him. Instead of fighting for what was rightfully his, Jacob decided

---

[4] Paraphrased Genesis 30: 26-36

[5] Paraphrased Genesis 30:26-36

[6] Paraphrased Genesis 30: 37:43

to take only a few (the spotted and speckled) and continue to work for Laban until he had enough (wealth) to go away on his own.

However, Jacob had a plan. He worked his plan, and that plan worked for him. Laban's herd began to reproduce kids which did not look like them. They reproduced spotted and speckled offspring like that which belonged to Jacob. As a result, Jacob's count increased and Laban's decreased significantly.[7]

Perhaps God has given you a dream of a better life, one in which money is never an issue. Maybe you have the same desire as Jacob, to obtain freedom from that 9 to 5 job that you are working where someone else is getting rich. "*He is able to do exceedingly abundantly above all that we ask or think, according to the power that works in us" (Ephesians 3:20).* The power that works in you is the Holy Spirit, which enables you to work the plan that God has given you. God wants us to be fruitful and to multiply.[8] Jacob's financial farming consisted of multiplying his resources. Make your money work for you, so you will not have to work so hard for it.

The Buddy System

Joan had no plan, because she did not maintain a budget. Joan's lack of planning allowed her to live far beyond her means. Had she monitored her expenditures, it would have caused her to exercise some self-control.

Maintaining a budget was where we suggested Joan begin reconstructing her life. We began here because rule number one at POTTS, International is, "Failing to plan means

---

[7] Paraphrased Genesis 31: 8-12

[8] Paraphrased Genesis 1:28

planning to fail." And up to this point, Joan's failure to plan had her on a collision course with certain disaster.

We taught Joan to look at her budget as her BUDdy that would help her GET her needs met and her goals achieved. Her budget helped her establish a spending plan that would assist her in regaining control of her life. The following were the steps we prescribed to bring Joan peace of mind:

1. Start tithing immediately to restore God's blessings in your life.

2. Cut up all credit cards to resist impulse shopping.

3. Pay off all debts once and for all.

4. Establish an emergency reserve by paying yourself second (after tithing)

5. Have 5% of your income deposited into your retirement account automatically.

Once Joan established these principles, she was well on her way to being transformed into a producer of wealth and not just a consumer. Let us now make clear the distinction between income and wealth. Income is what you make, and wealth is what you keep. We taught Joan how to keep income to produce wealth and not just to consume all of her resources. "Income requires that you continue to work either for someone else or yourself. Wealth is the accumulation of assets which create income for you."[9] Our biggest task was getting Joan beyond her fear of investing in the stock market.

Many people are afraid to invest in the stock market because they do not trust the system. They fear losing their money. They do not realize that they lose more by not investing in the market. George B. Thompson, founder of Millionaires in Training of Los Angeles, California, gives a wonderful demonstration of how the stock market works. He explains, "Almost everything you own is traded on the stock market." For example: You wake up in the morning and hit your alarm clock. The company that makes the clock is traded in the stock market. You roll out of bed, turning on the lamp on your nightstand. GE "Brings good things to light." General Electric is traded in the stock market. You go to the bathroom to shower. The water company, more than likely is traded in the stock market, and so are the companies that make your soap and shampoo. You brush your teeth, put on lotion and deodorant. The companies that make your tooth brush, tooth paste, lotion and deodorant of choice, also are traded in the stock market. You get dressed and the companies that made the clothes you wear are traded in the stock market. You have breakfast, more than likely what you are eating (Wheaties, Oatmeal or Pop Tarts), General Mills, Post or Kellogg's all are traded in the stock market. Finally, you get in your car, and yes the very automobile you drive and the tires you drive on are manufactured by companies which are traded in the stock market. "Therefore, you are participating in the market whether you realize it or not."[10]

---

[9] Kunjufu, Jawanza
1991 *Black Economics: Solutions for Economic and Community Empowerment*: African American Images Publishing: page 66
[10] Thompson, George B. Millionaires In Training: Los Angeles, CA

The problem is you are not making a profit from your participation.

The difference between your role and the role of an investor is you are a consumer and in most cases an over-consumer like Joan used to be. The investor is a producer of wealth, because his shares of stock represent ownership in the companies that sold him the shares. When these companies sell an alarm clock, light bulb, gallon of water, bar of soap, box of cereal or a car, their investors get paid. Your stock ownership translates into produced wealth. Now, as others spend their income on product consumption, you are building a solid future. This is the perfect example of financial farming. Congratulations!

Black Market, A Consuming Topic

Our client in this case study, Joan, is an African American. As African Americans, Rachelle and I are sensitive to the plight of minorities in the inner city. When we teach we encourage individuals to consider their wants versus their needs. "There is a rumor that African-Americans buy what they want and beg for what they need."[11] As much as it troubles me to do so, I must admit that there is some truth to this statement. (Remember Gimme Jimmy in Chapter 9)

The average American sees an estimated 2,000 advertising messages daily.[12] Unfortunately, "African-Americans are more likely to pay attention to advertising than any other group in America," according to Marilyn Kern-

---

[11] Kunjufu, Jawanza
1991 *Black Economics: Solutions for Economic and Community Empowerment*: African American Images Publishing: page 64

[12] Chapelle, Tony
1998 Emerge Magazine "Soul for Sale" January Issue: page 42

Foxworth, a journalism professor at Texas A&M University. Marketing specialists tend to agree with her.

Not only have advertising agencies gotten our attention, but they have gotten our money too. In 1997 it is estimated that African-Americans spent $469 billion.[13] We African-Americans are among the nation's leading consumers. And when it comes to clothes, "Black people spend more on clothing and related services than any other group."[14]

Marketing agencies are now using African-Americans and our culture to coax us into shopping. Thomas J. Burrell, chairman and CEO of the Burrell Communications Group, an African-American advertising agency in Chicago says, "We are not selling our souls when we use our culture in advertising...It's all about amassing capital. As a people, that's what we need to do. Our futures are about raising capital and eliminating the race-esteem deficit that exists in our communities." Mr. Burrell is correct on several accounts.

We do need to work toward amassing capital. We also need to address the self-esteem issue that exists in our communities. What we do not need, however, is to perpetuate the myth that self-esteem can be purchased! Self-esteem extends from understanding that *we were created in the image and likeness of God. Genesis 1:27*[15] The idea of championing mass consumerism as a viable means of economic empowerment is ridiculous. Perhaps Mr. Burrell's view is skewed by the fact that his company is among one of the few that benefit most from the billions being spent by African-American consumers.

There is an African-American apparel company called F.U.B.U. Apparently, this stands for "For Us, By Us." My

---

[13] Source: Selig Center for Economic Growth: University of Georgia.
[14] Packaged Facts, a New York based market research firm
1997 September "The African-American Market"
[15] Paraphrased Genesis 1:27

question still stands, How many of "Us" are truly benefiting? "Major publicly traded white-owned companies now have the lion's share of the market."[16] Our sports and entertainment figures are being utilized, "But, we are not in control...financially, or in the management and business aspect."[17]

Black to the Future

Rachelle and I emphatically stress to people that transforming their spending habits is vital to building a future that is not dictated by circumstances. We encourage our workshop attendees to take control of their future. Our personal testimony is often helpful.

Rachelle and I established a family budget shortly after we were married. Student loans were a substantial portion of our debt load. We retired nearly $100,000 of debt in approximately three years. Much of this debt elimination was achieved on one modest income! We reached this great goal by streamlining our monthly spending habits. We show others that 20 years of eating out, cable TV, junk food and shopping at the mall, siphon away what could have easily been $201,000 of accumulated wealth.*

---

[16] Chapelle, Tony
1998 Emerge Magazine "Soul for Sale" January Issue: page 46

[17] Chapelle, Tony
1998 Emerge Magazine "Soul for Sale" January Issue: page 46.

* This amount assumes the corresponding resources would have been invested on a monthly basis in a mutual fund yielding 8% annually.

Table 3: Shows what our wants really cost us.

Wants	True Cost
Eating out @ $30/wk.	$ 77,213
Cable TV @ $30/mo.	$ 17,818
Junk food @ $2/day	$ 38,607
Six Pack Soft drinks @ $3/wk.	$ 7,700
Shopping @ $100/mo.	$ 59,295
Total	$200,633

With the estimated $469 billion dollars African-Americans spent in 1997, we could have bought Microsoft twice! Microsoft was then and still is one of the three biggest corporations in the world.* Instead we bought: Versace, Rolex, Tommy Hilfiger, Nike and Mercedes Benz (depreciating assets). In the long run, we will have little or nothing to show for our hard-earned dollars. Failing to plan is planning to fail.

* Based on the value of shares outstanding (market capitalization)

Chapter 12

Establish Your Dynasty

Delay Gratification

...All my people shall be ruled according to your word...He became ruler over all the land of Egypt...without his consent no man could lift his hand or foot in all the land of Egypt. Genesis 41:40-44[1]

Now is an excellent time for review. We have covered many aspects of money. We do not want you to lose any crucial nuggets of information. However, we do want you to keep the subject matter in its proper perspective, so that you can fully comprehend the content.

We introduced and defined debtors prison. We outlined the origin, history and functions of money. We presented the misconceptions people develop about money and discussed each method of obtaining money. Last chapter, we distinguished between income and wealth and we also compared consuming and producing. This brings us up to current.

Hopefully, you can recall our evaluation of feast and famine minded individuals. The concept of feast and famine can be traced back to its origin in the book of Genesis. Abraham's great grandson, Joseph had the gift of interpreting dreams. Joseph's brothers resented him so much they threatened to kill him, but decided to sell him into slavery instead. Later, Joseph was tossed in prison for a crime he did not commit. However, a man that Joseph once helped

---

[1] Paraphrased Genesis 41:40-44

remembered his gift and brought him before Pharaoh, the king of Egypt.[2]

Pharaoh asked Joseph to interpret his dreams. He had two very disturbing dreams and none of his magicians could explain them. In the first dream Pharaoh saw seven cows, fat and sleek, come up out of the Nile and feed in the reed grass. Then seven other cows came up after them, poor, very ugly, and thin. The thin and ugly cows ate up the first seven fat cows, but when they had eaten them no one would have known that they had done so, for they were still as thin and ugly as before. In the second dream Pharaoh saw seven ears of grain, full and good, growing on one stalk, and seven ears withered thin, and blighted by the east wind, sprouting after them, and the thin ears swallowed up the seven good ears.[3]

Joseph explained to Pharaoh that his dreams were one and the same. He interpreted Pharaoh's dreams to mean that there would be seven years of feast, followed by seven years of famine. The famine would consume the land so much that the years of plenty would be forgotten. Joseph also explained to Pharaoh that dreaming this two consecutive times illustrated urgency, meaning this would happen very soon. Lastly, Joseph advised Pharaoh to take a fifth of the harvest during the seven feast years, to store in reserve to be used during the seven years of famine, so that Egypt would not be ruined. Pharaoh in turn placed Joseph, son of Israel, in charge of his entire kingdom.[4]

Joseph rose to great wealth and power because of his advice to delay gratification. As a result of this ingenious practice, Egypt became the mightiest empire in existence. Those seven years of famine ravaged the globe, so people traveled from all over the world to buy goods from the Egyptians. Delaying gratification definitely paid off.

---

[2] Genesis chapters 37-41

[3] Genesis 41:15-24

[4] Genesis 41:25-44

Delayed gratification is also the secret to building your personal empire and establishing a dynasty of economic abundance. You do not have to believe us, take the word of those who have done it. When it comes to the art of the deal, nobody is as famous as real-estate tycoon Donald Trump. Donald gives this smart money-saving advice: "Fight for the pennies and the dollars will come." Also, Money Mogul, Joe Dudley heads a multi-million dollar beauty empire and sticks to a budget. He says, "You must save money in order to have money. Buy what you can afford."[5]

Your question may be, "I do not know if I can do this? How do I delay gratification? I do not have any will power." You are not alone in your doubts. In Romans 7:14-24, Apostle Paul expressed similar concerns. Let us observe his dilemma. "I do not understand what I do. For what I want to do I do not do, but what I hate I do...nothing good lives in me...For I have the desire to do what is good, but I cannot carry it out. For what I do is not the good I want to do; no the evil I do not want to do - this I keep on doing...When I want to do good, evil is right there with me...What a wretched man I am! Who will rescue me..."[6] Does this sound familiar? Paul traces the problem of self-control to the power of sin. The content of that sin power remains active in our thoughts and actions. We, like Paul, have a hard time controlling some of our own behavior.[7] Despite Paul's challenges, he accomplished great feats for the sake of the gospel. In fact, Paul is given credit for writing nearly half of the books in the New Testament.

---

[5] Oprah Winfrey Show
2000 Money Saving Secrets aired 04/28/00: Harpo Productions

[6] Romans 7:14-24 New International Version

[7] Backus, William Dr.
1987 *Finding The Freedom Of Self-Control: Life-Changing Answers to "I Can't Help It! I Can't Say No! I Can't Control Myself!"* Bethany House Publishers: Minneapolis, MN: page 19

Conquering Self

We live in a world where 'instant gratification' prevails. Dr. William Backus calls this the "I want it and I want it now" culture. The good doctor is right on point. This microwave society we live in has negatively affected our character. Today, every person in the western world (and much of the third world as well) is exposed forcefully and repeatedly to the message that restraint is neither necessary nor good. Our mass media says we will miss many important things in life unless we learn how to let impulses, emotions, and desires have free reign.[8]

The media that entices us to spend more than we earn; to buy that new, over-priced car we cannot afford, to mortgage our homes and lease our self esteem, does not explain where this free flowing attitude will leave us. This pattern of behavior is a first-class ticket to despair. This very popular road leads many down the path of destruction. "*Enter by the narrow gate; for wide is the gate and broad is the way that leads to destruction, and there are many who go by it. Because narrow is the gate and difficult is the way which leads to life, there are few who find it" (Matthew 7:13,14).* Change directions now. Do not take the wrong road. You have everything to lose and nothing to gain. Learn from the tragic example of those who lived before you. Peter the Great, the "Czar of All the Russians" merited the title "Great." But he was subject to fits of rage and, in one of these outbursts, he killed his own son. Toward the end of his life, Peter the Great said, "I have conquered an empire, but I was not able to conquer myself."[9] A fruit of the Spirit is self-control.[10]

---

[8] Backus, William Dr.
1987 *Finding the Freedom Of Self-Control*: Bethany House Publishers: Minneapolis, MN: page 19
[9] Backus, Williamd Dr.

Baby Steps

You can delay gratification. Just take it one step at a time. This response may appear cliche, but it is true. A wise man once said, "The journey of a thousand miles begins with just one step." Another said, "The only way to eat an elephant is one bite at a time." Although it seems to be an insurmountable task, you can do it. We are certain of this. You do not have to take this journey alone. You have a companion with you to encourage you when times get tough. God himself accompanies you in this quest. "*And the Lord, He is the One who goes before you. He will be with you, He will not leave you nor forsake you; do not fear nor be dismayed" (Deuteronomy 31:9).* Just stay on course and do not give up. Jesus said, *Lo, I am with you always, even to the end of the age (Matthew 28:20).*[11]

We do not deny the fact that saving and delaying gratification is a sacrifice. However, this sacrifice will ultimately benefit your bottom line. The children of Israel developed a custom of making sacrificial offerings to God. These sacrifices usually brought God's blessing upon their lives. He appreciated seeing selflessness and self-control in his chosen people, and he still does.

Webster's defines *sacrifice* as the giving up of one thing for the sake of another.[12] God the Father obviously believes in this practice, because He made the ultimate sacrifice. He gave His only Son, so that we might be saved. "*For God so loved the world that He gave His only begotten*

1987 Finding The Freedom Of Self-Control: Bethany House Publishers: Minneapolis, MN: page 21

[10] Paraphrased Galatians 5:22,23

[11] Paraphrased Matthew 28:20

[12] *Webster's Collegiate Dictionary*
1981 G. & C. Merrim Company: Springfield, Massachusetts

Son, that whosoever believeth in him should not perish, but have everlasting life" (John 3:16). [13] Surely, God will honor your sacrifice also.

[13] John 3:16, King James Version

Epilogue

We have provided all of the tools you need to master your money. The principles herein are tried and true. If you adopt them, you will prosper.

It is our prayer that the people this book reaches will accept Christ as their Lord and Savior. If you do not know Him, invite Him into your life today. If you do know Him, work on developing a closer, more intimate relationship with Him. Spend time with Him everyday, just as you would your best friend. For He is a friend who sticks closer than a brother.[1] Apostle John exclaimed, "*Greater love has no man than this, that a man lay down his life for his friends" (John 15:13).*

Do not desire to become rich solely for the sake of being rich. There is a purpose for your money, just as there is a purpose for your life. Our money has a mission. The Bible admonishes, *Remember the Lord thy God: for it is he who gives you the ability to produce wealth to confirm his covenant which he swore to your forefathers, as it is this day.*[2] Do you desire wealth for the right reasons? Jesus exhorts, "For where your treasure is, there your heart will be also."[3] God knows your heart. He judges the thoughts, attitudes and intentions of the heart.[4]

If you are wondering about your true motives for pursuing wealth, this will help you. We once heard a

---

[1] Paraphrased Proverbs 18:24

[2] Paraphrased Deuteronomy 8:18 New International Version

[3] Luke 12:34

[4] Paraphrased Hebrews 4:12 New International Version

preacher explain that there are two items in everyone's possession that clearly identify what is most important to that individual: his calendar and his checkbook. Where do you spend most of your time? And, where do you spend most of your money? Your answers, of course, should be with God.

Another great method of discovering whether or not you have money in its proper perspective is to ask yourself, "Would I give it all up?" Ironically, we have spent this entire book examining how to get money, how to keep money and how to grow money, only to tell you now that you must be willing to give it all up.

There were two men in the bible who failed this most crucial test. Observe the Parable of the Rich Fool: *Jesus said, "Watch out! Be on your guard against all kinds of greed; a man's life does not consist in the abundance of his possessions. The ground of a certain rich man produced a good crop. He thought to himself, 'What shall I do? I have no place to store my crops.' Then he said, 'This is what I'll do. I will tear down my barns and build bigger ones, and there I will store all my grain and my goods. And I'll say to myself "You have plenty of good things laid up for many years. Take life easy; eat, drink and be merry"' (Luke 12:15-19)*[5]

But God said to him, 'You fool! This very night your soul will be required of you."[6]

Similarly, we find the Parable of the Rich Ruler in Luke 18:18-24. Jesus told this gentleman, *"You still lack one thing. Sell everything you have and give it to the*

---

[5] Luke 12:15-19 New International Version

[6] Luke 12:20 New International Version

poor...Then come, follow me." When he heard this, he became very sad, because he was a man of great wealth.[7]

Money is very important, but money is not everything. For what will it profit a man, if he gains the whole world but loses his own soul? Or, what shall a man give in exchange for his soul?[8] You must be willing to give it all up, no questions asked, if that is what God wants you to do. Never forget that we do not love money, we love God. *"For the love of money is the root of all evil" (1 Timothy 6:10).*[9]

We agree with Apostle John concerning you; *Beloved I pray that you may prosper in all things and be in health just as you soul prospers" (3 John 2).* May God richly bless you! Amen.

---

[7] Luke 18:22,23 New International Version
[8] Matthew 6:26 King James Version
[9] 1 Timothy 6:10 King James Version

About the Authors

Minister Tyrone Potts has been a *'business man'* more than twenty-five years. Though born to a large family of modest means, Tyrone envisioned more. He opened his first bank account at age six, then his entrepreneurial spirit soared. Tyrone established his first profitable business at eight-years-old. At age twelve, he began investing. After obtaining a degree in Business Administration from Georgetown University, Tyrone became a Certified Public Accountant and worked for one of the top five accounting firms in the world. More than ten years of experience in both public and private accounting credits his expertise in business and finance.

Rachelle Potts is a licensed Evangelist Missionary. She obtained a social science degree from Dillard University and attended Loyola University School of Law. Rachelle is a mediator for the Los Angeles County Bar Association and an arbitrator for the Council of Better Business Bureaus. She specializes in resolving business and finance related conflicts. Rachelle has reconciled the discrepancies of corporate clients in the banking industry. Employed as both a stockbroker and a fund-raiser, she's spent her career working for financial institutions and undertaking fiscal affairs at non-profits.

The Potts are anointed for their assignment to economically empower people. Their financial backgrounds and professional experiences contribute to their mastery of money, uniquely qualifying them to revolutionize the way we view our resources. The Potts teach from first-hand experience. They also practice what they preach: eliminating nearly $100,000 of debt in three years on one income and retiring at ages 32 and 29. The Potts live off investment income and strive to empower others. They recently released the first two books of the Escape From Debtors Prison series, *Got Money?* and *Let My People Go! Debt-Proof Shopping*, third book in the series will be released in November 2001.

Prosperity Outpouring To The Saints, Intl.

POTTS, International is a ministry designed to educate the masses about stewardship, while providing products and much needed business services to those who are committed to learning the principles of sound money management. Tyrone and Rachelle Potts believe that God's prosperity should pour out to the saints across the globe. They founded POTTS, Intl. to conduct conferences, seminars and workshops around the world. POTTS, Intl. provides the biblical foundation and practical application of abundant Christian living.

POTTS, Intl. teaches people how to get out and stay out of debt. Other organizations adopt a notion of good debt versus bad debt. However, Prosperity Outpouring To The Saints, Intl. has a no debt policy that honors scripture. Apostle Paul said, Owe no man nothing but to love. And Deuteronomy 28:12 reads, *"We shall not borrow."* Thus, believers should not be in debt. For the borrower is enslaved.

Webster's defines "debt" as sin, trespass, an actionable state of owing and a "debtor" as one guilty of neglect or violation of duty. POTTS, International's debt-free foundational premise shows people how to concentrate on serving God according to His calling, not money. It also provides a road map for financial independence. The mission of POTTS, Intl. is "To set the financial captives free." This mission begins with Christians but is geared toward liberating all mankind. Financial freedom is a vital part of the wholeness which operating in obedience to God brings.

POTTS, Intl. offers financial planning, investment coaching and debt counseling services. Take this debt-free message to your congregation, business organization, book club or investment group. Contact POTTS, Intl., P.O. Box 13921, Torrance, CA 90503 or email: hisfavor@aol.com, regarding presentations or products. Visit the POTTS, Intl. website: www.prosperityoutpouring.qpg.com. for details.

Prosperity Outpouring To The Saints, Intl.

Post Office Box 13921 Torrance, CA 90503 (310)542-5001 email: hisfavor@aol.com
www.prosperityoutpouring.qpg.com

Product Description	Quantity	Unit Price
Family Budget & Debt Priority Payoff Plan Software that helps you manage your money and get out of debt.		**40.00**
Get Out Of Debt Presentation Packet A hard copy of the information taught in the seminar.		**20.00**
Powerful Principles of Prosperity Framed 5'7" plaque of the commandments for success.		**12.00**
Got MONEY? 5'7" plaque of benefits & drawbacks to money-making methods.		**12.00**
Power Rx Scriptural cure for common problems that hold back our blessings.		**8.00**
Double Dose Combined Prosperity Principles or Got MONEY? with Power Rx		**17.00**
Escape From Debtors Prison: Got MONEY? 200 page book about the 8 various methods of obtaining money.		**18.00**
90 minute Audio Cassette *God's Success Formula* establishes the biblical basis for abundance.		**10.00**
4 hour Audio Cassette Presentation *Budgeting, Debt Elimination, Stock Investing & Intro to Estate Planning*		**20.00**

Shipping & Handling $3.95 per unit

Subtotal ______ ________

* Optional....Love gifts and offerings are also appreciated. (not tax deductible) ________

TOTAL ________

Name______________________________

Address_________________________City___________State___Zip_____

Yes ________ include me on your mailing list for seminars, products and prayer.

Prosperity Outpouring To The Saints, Intl.

Post Office Box 13921 Torrance, CA 90503 (310)542-5001 email: hisfavor@aol.com
www.prosperityoutpouring.qpg.com

Product Description	Quantity	Unit Price
Family Budget & Debt Priority Payoff Plan Software that helps you manage your money and get out of debt.		**40.00**
Get Out Of Debt Presentation Packet A hard copy of the information taught in the seminar.		**20.00**
Powerful Principles of Prosperity Framed 5'7" plaque of the commandments for success.		**12.00**
Got MONEY? 5'7" plaque of benefits & drawbacks to money-making methods.		**12.00**
Power Rx Scriptural cure for common problems that hold back our blessings.		**8.00**
Double Dose Combined Prosperity Principles or Got MONEY? with Power Rx		**17.00**
Escape From Debtors Prison: Got MONEY? 200 page book about the 8 various methods of obtaining money.		**18.00**
90 minute Audio Cassette *God's Success Formula* establishes the biblical basis for abundance.		**10.00**
4 hour Audio Cassette Presentation *Budgeting, Debt Elimination, Stock Investing & Intro to Estate Planning*		**20.00**

Shipping & Handling $3.95 per unit

Subtotal _______ ________

* Optional....Love gifts and offerings are also appreciated. (not tax deductible) __________

TOTAL __________

Name____

Address________________________________City____________State___Zip_____

Yes ________ include me on your mailing list for seminars, products and prayer.